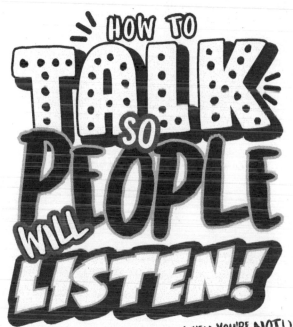

HOW TO TALK SO PEOPLE WILL LISTEN!

(AND SOUND **CONFIDENT** EVEN WHEN YOU'RE **NOT!**)

For anyone who ever feels awkward

speaking out loud.

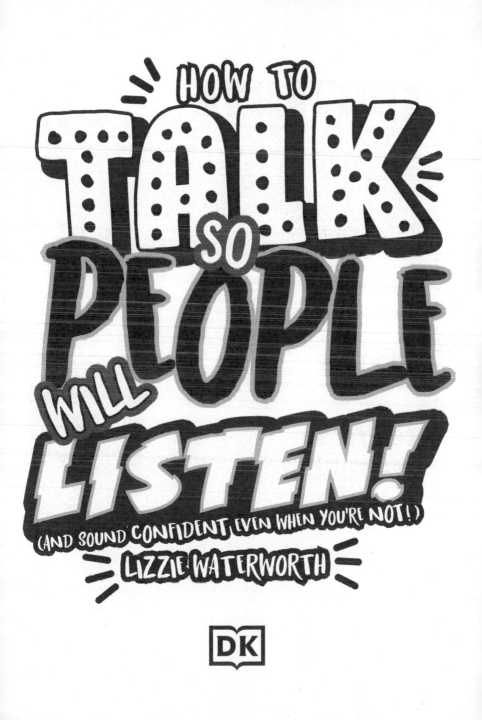

CONTENTS

Introduction 7

CHAPTER 1
Tame your nerves 16

CHAPTER 2
Help them hear you 48

CHAPTER 3
Train, don't strain 72

CHAPTER 4
Connection! Is anybody out there? 132

CHAPTER 5
Cool, confident you 164

Glossary 170

HI, I'M LIZZIE WATERWORTH.

It's likely you've heard me before, even if you haven't heard my name. That's because I'm the voice of many characters in TV cartoons and video games and commercials and even toys. The hundreds of characters I've voiced include: Henry from *Horrid Henry* (he's really Horrid!), Spider from *Superworm*, Ricky from *DinoCity*, Alfred in David Walliams' *Beast of Buckingham Palace*, Bolly and Miff from *Mush-Mush and the Mushables*, Bello from *Jelly Jamm*, Uniqua and Austin in *The Backyardigans*...

I LIVE IN A WORLD OF CARTOONS, AND I LOVE MY JOB.

To do it well, I need to sound confident and read lines in lots of different voices without making lots of mistakes. Think this comes easily to me? Think again! The truth is, no one is born with a natural ability to do these things effortlessly. I'm still learning all the time, and sometimes I lose my confidence.

We all get **NERVOUS.** That's why I've written this book. I want to tell you the crazy truth about my world of voicing cartoons. So, the next time you feel stressed about talking to someone new, or panic about speaking in front of the class, or forget your lines in the school play and think all your friends will be laughing at you, and you feel your confidence level drop to 0/10, you can reach for your confidence toolbox! I'll explain what this is later.

But first, let me tell you a story. I'd been voicing cool characters in cartoons for a few years when I got a call from my voiceover agent.

> LIZZIE, YOU HAVE AN AUDITION FOR A BRAND-NEW CARTOON. THE JOB WOULD BE IN IRELAND, AND ALL YOUR TRAVEL AND FLIGHT COSTS WOULD BE PAID FOR.

Exciting! The idea of taking a plane to work sounded like a vacation!

> THERE ARE TWO CHARACTERS YOU NEED TO AUDITION FOR. ONE IS A FEISTY TEENAGE GIRL, AND THE OTHER IS HER GRANDMA, WHO'S ABOUT 90 YEARS OLD. THE AUDITION IS IN TWO DAYS. I'LL SEND THE SCRIPTS TO YOU NOW.

A note on the script said the girl should have an American accent. So, after practicing and having fun with the script, I was ready for my "teenage girl" audition.

CONFIDENCE LEVEL 10/10!

Next, it was time to practice the grandmother's voice. I opened my mouth and started reading. But instead of sounding like a 90-year-old lady, I sounded like I had a crackly sore throat. Oh no, the audition was the next day! I kept reading the lines over and over, trying a high voice, then a lower voice ... but I wasn't even close to getting this old lady voice right.

While traveling into central London, I was conscious of the other train passengers staring at me as I croaked quietly, trying to channel my inner grandma. When I arrived at the studio, they took me straight through to a voice booth—a little soundproof room where cartoon voiceovers are recorded—and they introduced me to the director.

HEY LIZZIE, LET'S START WITH THE GIRL'S VOICE, SHALL WE?

I gave it my best shot:

DAD, I DON'T WANNA BE ON VACATION IN THE WOODS, THERE'S, LIKE, ANIMAL POOP AROUND THAT WILL RUIN MY NEW SNEAKERS. WHAT DID I JUST STEP IN—EUGHH! AND THERE'S NO CELL PHONE CHARGER. HOW AM I GOING TO CONTACT MY FRIENDS?

GREAT, LIZZIE,

said the director,

OK, LET'S MOVE ON TO GRANDMA'S VOICE.

This was the moment I had been dreading.

CONFIDENCE LEVEL 3/10.

I tried to say, "Come on, dear," but what came out was the voice of a malfunctioning robot. My old-lady voice was a disaster. I hadn't even finished my lines before the director interrupted with "OK, thanks, Lizzie, you can go."

Never in my years of auditioning had I not even been allowed to finish the lines. I felt sick to my stomach.

As I scuttled out of the voice booth, tiny tears formed in the corners of my eyes. By the time I reached the train station, the tears had grown into huge, fat sobs. That's right: I had begun **THE UNCONTROLLABLE CRY.** You know the one I'm talking about. Once you start, you can't stop, no matter what. You just have to let it run. Only it usually happens in the privacy of your home, or the school restrooms, not at London Waterloo station—one of the busiest train stations in the UK! **CRINGE!**

Eventually, The Uncontrollable Cry subsided. Phew! But my ordeal wasn't over yet. I began the "what if" thinking. "What if" thinking is like having an annoying little imaginary creature jumping on your shoulder when you're not feeling your best, and it starts

whispering unhelpful words into your ears, which makes you start doubting yourself even more. The little creature (let's call it Whatif) jumps on you when your confidence drops below 0% and your imagination climbs up to 100%, and it makes you feel much worse!

THIS IS WHAT MISCHIEVOUS LITTLE WHATIF STARTED WHISPERING...

> What if right now, that director is on the phone to your voiceover agent, saying, "How could you let that girl audition, she's wasted my time, and time is money!" Or, even worse, what if he's going through his contacts, calling every director in the country, saying, "Never book Lizzie Waterworth for a job. She's a disgrace to this industry!

... and so it went, on and on. Pesky little Whatif just wouldn't get off my shoulder!

Needless to say, I didn't get that job.

I've told you this true story because, even though I've been voicing for so long, I still sometimes feel like I've messed up in an audition or made a fool of myself in front of people—people who expect me to get it right. I'm sure you have your own examples of things not going the way you'd hoped. At the time, it might have felt really bad, and, like me, you may have felt upset.

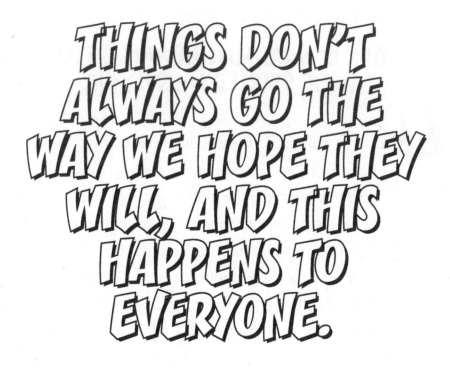

THINGS DON'T ALWAYS GO THE WAY WE HOPE THEY WILL, AND THIS HAPPENS TO EVERYONE.

Ever since the grandma voice disaster, I carry my **CONFIDENCE TOOLBOX** with me at all times. This isn't an actual box; it's a collection of cool tricks to help me feel more positive, and I want to share it with you in this book. You can use this box of tricks anytime you feel your own confidence level dropping.

14

I have lots of fun stories to tell you. Some are about my crazy life in cartoons—like the time I really embarrassed myself in front of Sir David Attenborough. Others are true tales about other people, many of whom are famous now but have had to work hard to overcome their fear of public speaking and performing. Oh, and I've even recruited some of my fellow voice artists and other friends from the world of cartoons to share their tips, tricks, and ideas to help with confident speaking.

LET'S GET GOING!

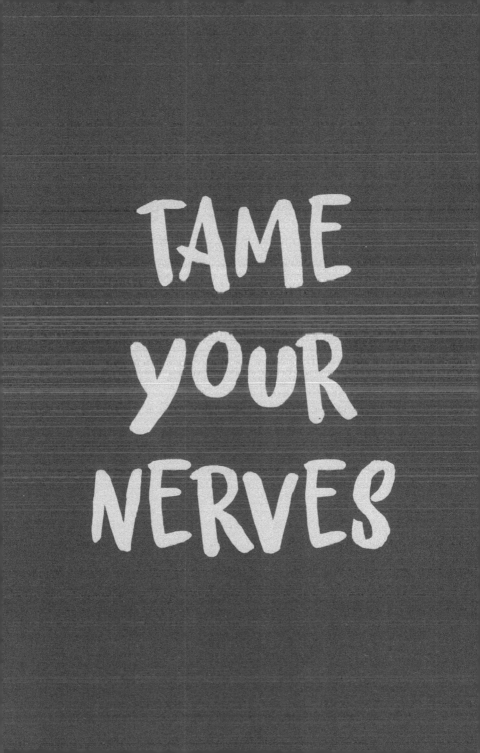

FIRST, LET'S TALK ABOUT TAMING THOSE PESKY NERVES.

Do you ever feel little pangs of worry and fear before speaking out loud in front of the class or even a teacher? Yep, me too! And sometimes several weird feelings come along at the same time, which can make you feel a little yucky. **WHY DOES THIS HAPPEN?** I asked Jenny Clarke, a family counselor (aka someone who's good at helping people deal with worries), and this is what she said.

"Lizzie, you know how much you love rollercoaster rides and how much I DON'T love them. If you and I were both at the start of a rollercoaster ride together, we would both be feeling lots of things in our bodies. Maybe some tingles in our arms and legs, maybe a bit sick, maybe a bit hot or cold, even a little bit sweaty, our hearts beating faster—perhaps some fluttering butterflies in our tummies as well. I would be feeling very scared and dreading the ride, and you would be feeling excited and looking forward to the ride. But we would both be experiencing the same things in our bodies.

THE DIFFERENCE IS IN OUR HEADS.

"Your brain would tell you it's because you're incredibly excited, and my brain would tell me it's because I'm scared."

"It's our brain—that little voice inside us—that tells us what our feelings mean. So, next time you think you feel scared, remember, you would feel exactly the same in your body if you were excited about something, and this might help you relax."

Someone who knows all about this is the awesome actress Emma Tate, who voices Henry's little brother, Perfect Peter. Let's hear from her...

TIPS FROM THE TOP

EMMA TATE

ACTRESS

Hi, I'm Emma Tate. I've acted on stage, TV, radio, in video games, and played hundreds of characters in cartoons, including Peter in *Horrid Henry*.

I used to be so shy that I was often too afraid to speak and would stumble and trip over my words. But then I discovered that if I was doing something that really interested me, I was able to find my voice. I still sometimes get butterflies in my stomach, but now instead of thinking of that rush of adrenaline as being fear, I think of it as being **EXCITEMENT** that gives me energy. I remember to stand up straight, make eye contact, and smile. And I automatically look, sound, and feel more confident and in control. The more you speak up, the easier it gets. And if I can do it, so can you. *GOOD LUCK!*

WHAT A GREAT FIRST TIP TO ADD TO OUR CONFIDENCE TOOLBOX.

So, it seems this rush of **YUCKY** feelings we get when we're nervous is normal (phew!). We call these feelings "nerves," but I like to call them "spark-zaps" because they can make your body react in all sorts of odd ways. Some people get flushed cheeks, and other people start biting their nails or stuttering over their words. We sometimes feel out of control when the spark-zaps are whizzing and buzzing around inside us.

Despite being "normal," the spark-zaps can be very annoying, and, like hiccups, they can happen to us just when we least expect them. I've been to more than a hundred auditions, but I can still get nervous!

A few years ago, I was asked to perform extra voices on the famous *Snail and the Whale* film, adapted by the BBC from Julia Donaldson's excellent book. It had a cast of famous celebrities, and I got a call at the last minute to come in and record the extra voices.

I turned up to the studio, feeling pretty confident, but then I walked into the voice booth and heard:

Suddenly, I felt those spark-zapping nerves kick into action! What does a snail even sound like?!

PANIC ON BOARD.

Whatif climbed on my shoulder and started whispering, "What if you don't sound like a snail? What if you sound more like a bird?" Those annoying little spark-zappers were buzzing all over me. Suddenly, my body felt very funny. I was biting my nails, and my hands were **SHAKING.** My breathing grew faster. My cheeks seemed hot, and my head felt like it was about to explode.

FUN FACT

We all have cells called **NEURONS** that spend their days sending messages around our bodies. They send messages between our brain, our skin, our organs, our glands, and our muscles. These are not messages like text messages; they're nerve signals. It's the spark-zaps at work! But this time, they are being helpful—allowing us to move our limbs and feel things that keep us safe, such as feeling too hot when we blow out a candle on a birthday cake and get too close to the flame. Thank your spark-zap nerves for keeping you from getting burned!

In this chapter, I'm going to share some tips from my confidence toolbox that helped me calm the spark-zappers when I was **FREAKING OUT** that day about my snail voice and little Whatif was dancing on my head!

TIP NUMBER 1: TRY BELLY BREATHING

Some great advice about "belly breathing" was given to me by Mel Churcher, a voice expert who's worked with lots of different actors. Let's breathe with her...

"Hello, I'm Mel Churcher. I work with actors of all ages. I have helped actors ride dragons and be time bandits. It's very important to be able to breathe easily when you work on your speech, and posture is a very important part of that. Let's try a little experiment together. Sit normally, shut your eyes, put your hand on your stomach, and allow yourself to breathe in and out into your hand. As you breathe in, your tummy gets bigger, and then it goes back as you breathe out. Can you feel that? That's relaxed breathing. Now, next part of our experiment. Lift your shoulders high up to your ears. **CAN YOU FEEL HOW THAT AFFECTS YOUR BREATHING?** Can you breathe? I don't think you can breathe easily. Let your shoulders go.

Now, hunch forward as if you are looking at something that you don't like below you on the table. Can you breathe? No, not really. Sit back up like normal. Now, stick your chin out. Can you breathe at all? It's really hard, isn't it? So, you want to find yourself back with your relaxed normal posture. Imagine at the top of your head there is a golden string taking you up to the sky. Let your shoulders be really relaxed. Allow yourself to just fill the space. Now, you are breathing easily."

Here are some more tips for practicing relaxed breathing from Dr. Natalie Cawley, who is a counseling psychologist and psychotherapist:

 Close your eyes. Imagine you are holding a lemon in each hand.

 Squeeze those lemons as hard as you can! Squeeze, squeeze, squeeze... Squeeze that last drop of juice out!

 Now, drop the lemons.

 Breathe in and out deeply. As you breathe, fill your belly up with air and then push all the air back out.

 Try this three more times.

Now, you know how to find your relaxed breath when you're feeling **NERVOUS** or **SHAKY.** These exercises can make you feel instantly more relaxed. They will also really warm your voice up so that when the words come out, they should already feel more projected, making you sound CLEARER and more CONFIDENT!

SO, YAY FOR BELLY BREATHING!

You can do belly breathing anytime you feel anxious or uneasy, and it could help you relax and feel more in control. **FUN FACT**—If you ask most people to take a deep breath, they'll lift their chest and suck their breath in. This is because they don't think about how they breathe when they are relaxed. That means they automatically go into what we call **FIGHT-OR-FLIGHT** mode, which is our bodies' way of responding to a stressful situation. When you're under stress, sometimes your body will react as if you're about to either fight something or run away from it! This can make us tense up. But unless you are about to fight a lion or run away from it, do your natural belly breathing to help yourself feel relaxed!

TIP NUMBER 2: SLOW DOWN

Helping yourself feel relaxed before speaking makes such a difference.

ALLOW YOURSELF A BRIEF TIME-OUT,

says my friend and cartoon voice actor Marcel.

MARCEL MCCALLA

VOICEOVER ARTIST

Hi, I'm Marcel McCalla, and I'm a voiceover artist. I voice numbers 2, 4, and 8 in the CBeebies series *Numberblocks*. For me, sometimes words tend to jump around a bit. So, what I like to do is slow my breathing, ground myself, and take my time. Hey, the world is in too much of a rush anyway.

Taking a few minutes to ground yourself and give your mind a moment to calm down can also be helpful in many other situations that make us tense, scared, or overwhelmed.

TIP NUMBER 3: STOP THE SHAKES

Nerves sometimes make your hands shake, which can feel a bit weird. This happened to me once when I was holding a piece of paper with a speech written on it. **ONE MINUTE I WAS READING AND IT WAS TOTALLY FINE,** then suddenly my hands began randomly shaking and the paper was wobbling about all over the place. Later, when I looked into this, I found that shaking hands is actually a pretty common response to nerves. It's because when we feel stressed, stress hormones can cause our muscles to tense, which can lead to **TREMBLING** or **SHAKING.**

Sometimes, we get a tremor in our voices, too, but more on that later. For now, what do we have in the Confidence Toolbox for random and uncontrollable hand-shaking before giving a speech?

FIRST, SHAKE THE SHAKES OUT!

It might sound strange, but instead of letting the shakes shake you up, deliberately shaking your hands yourself could actually help them wake up a bit and calm those nerves!

Next, if you're reading your speech from a piece of paper or a tablet and the shakes begin, hold the corners, not the middle.

THIS WILL

 help your body feel more in control of your notes.

 help you feel more balanced, so your hands shouldn't shake as much.

 make your audience less likely to see your hands if they still shake because they're spread out.

 make you less likely to drop your paper or tablet.

And whatever you do, don't listen to Whatif (Yes, Whatif, it's time for a nap!).

TIP NUMBER 4: BANISH THOSE BLUSHES

I spoke to Freya, age 11, who told me:

The increased color in our cheeks is officially called **BLUSHING.** According to Professor Mark Leary, blushing is a reaction to **UNDESIRED SOCIAL ATTENTION** and is a way of deflecting it (or turning away from it). It doesn't just happen when we speak in front of other people. According to Professor Leary, you can turn red just by opening presents when people are looking at you.

SO, WHAT CAN WE DO TO MANAGE THESE ANNOYING BLUSHES? These are tools that have helped me and lots of other people.

 Blushing tends to happen more when you're feeling warm. So, keep yourself **COOL** by removing a layer of clothing if you can or having a cold drink, ideally water, to keep the body working as it should.

 **CLOSE YOUR EYES** for a few seconds and think of something that makes you feel relaxed, maybe chilling in your living room or somewhere you've been on vacation. Then, open your eyes again. This gives you a few seconds to **REBOOT** and hopefully calm the blush down.

SMILE! This will help relax your face and hopefully calm down those nerve-zaps. And this will make whomever you're talking to more relaxed too!

HOW TO MANAGE LEG-SHAKES

If you feel your legs shaking, try to spread your feet wider apart. This will help you feel more **STABLE** and **STRONGER** than if your legs were together.

Now seems the perfect time to include a brilliant tip about this from actor David Menkin...

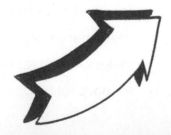

TIPS FROM THE TOP

DAVID MENKIN

ACTOR

I'm David Menkin, and you might know me as Luke Skywalker in *LEGO Star Wars* and lots of other games and cartoons. Now, my top tip is **ANCHORING.** You know, like how a ship drops anchor so it doesn't float away? Well, you can do that too! When you're standing up in front of people, sometimes you can feel like you want to run away, right? Well, to help you feel secure and ready to be listened to, make sure your legs are planted on the ground. Go on, stamp them on the floor a couple of times. It's amazing how great you sound when you have a really good foundation.

SO, DROP THAT ANCHOR!

LET'S ANCHOR THIS TIP IN OUR
CONFIDENCE TOOLBOX!

SPEAKING WITH A STUTTER

To *stutter* means "to speak with an involuntary repetition of certain sounds," particularly sounds that go at the beginning of each word. **ACCORDING TO THE STUTTERING FOUNDATION, MORE THAN 80 MILLION PEOPLE STUTTER.**

That's a lot of people! So, if you have a stutter, you're not on your own.

Ten-year-old Lewis has a stutter and knows all too well how frustrating it can be. He has this great tip to share.

HI, MY NAME IS LEWIS. I HAVE A STUTTER. TO MAKE ME FEEL MORE CONFIDENT WHEN I TALK, I TRY TO SLOW DOWN AND CALM MYSELF DOWN.

THANKS, LEWIS! Not only good advice but helpful openness too. The more we open up to other people with things we find difficult, the more we learn about each other and how to help each other.

If you know somebody who stammers or stutters, now you know to give them the time they need to speak. Well done, Lewis, for speaking up and speaking out!

YOU HAVE YOUR OWN SUPERPOWER!

Have you ever heard your favorite music artist or band play a musical instrument so well that it seems like they were born to play it? Music stars often have access to the best musical instruments and then, after practicing (a lot), they sound great! You can do this too. You already have your own instrument!

YOU HAVE YOUR OWN UNIQUE VOICE.

This amazing instrument allows you to make sounds and words through your mouth. And we're so used to using our voice every day that it's easy to forget its

AMAZING POWER.

Occasionally, we get sick and can't speak properly, like when we have a sore throat. When this happens, we say we have lost our voice.

UGH, WHATIF, WHAT ARE YOU DOING HERE?

"Well, what if the next time you lose your voice, you never get it back? Or..."

OH, WHATIF, I REALLY DON'T HAVE TIME FOR YOU RIGHT NOW!

BACK TO WHAT I WAS SAYING...

As an actor who voices cartoons, I'd be lost without my voice. Using my voice to read a script is essential. It's only when I lose the power to talk out loud that I appreciate how much I rely on it. Without my voice, I wouldn't be able to shout Henry's classic line

Of course, my voice could be replaced by another actor's voice, but no one could speak as my cartoon character exactly the same way I do. We all have our own, unique voice. Your voice is as unique as your fingerprint!

As Henry would say,

When you press a piano key with your finger, it makes a sound. The same thing happens when we use our voice! But how? And does it really matter if we know how it works? The answer is YES! **ONCE WE KNOW HOW OUR VERY OWN INSTRUMENT WORKS, WE CAN GET REALLY GOOD AT USING IT.**

MEET LARRY THE LARYNX!

We all have a little box inside our throats. People often call it a voice box, but officially it's called the larynx. We need it to breathe and speak. It's the little lump you can feel and see at the front of your neck.

I call mine Larry. It stores folds of tissue called vocal chords or vocal folds, which create the sounds. With me so far?

Let me introduce you to Larry. Take a deep breath to relax your body. Then, take your finger and position it on the front of your neck and say, **"HELLO, LARRY."** You should feel it vibrating a bit – **THIS IS LARRY!**

Now, do a pretend yawn! This will help you relax before you start speaking and make your vocal cords loosen up for **INCREASED COMFORT AND CONFIDENCE.**

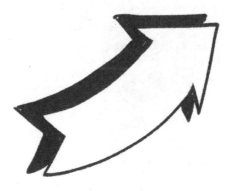

I CAN'T STRESS HOW MUCH IT HELPS TO FEEL CHILLED OUT WHEN YOU'RE TRYING TO SHARE IMPORTANT INFORMATION OR DO A PRESENTATION AT SCHOOL. YOU GET WHAT YOU'RE SAYING ACROSS IN THE BEST WAY.

SOUND IS PRODUCED WHEN AIR PASSES THROUGH YOUR VOCAL CORDS,

causing them to vibrate and create sound waves in the nose, mouth, and pharynx (that's a little tube inside your neck). Pretty cool! Your voice's pitch (how high or low it sounds) is determined by the amount of tension on your vocal cords. So, for example, if I were asked to voice an alien in a video game, I would put a lot of tension on my vocal cords to change the sound to an alien voice.

The famous actor and presenter Stephen Fry (whom you may know as the narrator of the *Harry Potter* audiobooks in the UK) has a couple of **FANTASTIC** tips about this. Not only does Stephen have to project his voice in front of people and cameras on TV, but he also talks to **HUGE AUDIENCES** when he hosts big award ceremonies! I bumped into Stephen at a recording studio when I was writing this book. **I KNOW, WHAT ARE THE CHANCES OF THAT HAPPENING, EH?**

I told him what the book is about and he kindly gave us a couple of exclusive top tips for **THE CONFIDENCE TOOLBOX!** Take it away Stephen...

★ TIPS FROM THE TOP ★

STEPHEN FRY
ACTOR, PRESENTER

Hello, Stephen Fry here. Now, what's the best tip I can think of for vocal production? Well, I suppose the thing that's most important is not to **HURRY** or to be **STRAINED. LET YOUR THROAT RELAAAAAAAAAAX** and just allow your voice to have its own quality. Don't try to do an impression of someone else's voice.

BE YOURSELF! Even if you think your own voice is silly, others won't. So, just enjoy the moment of letting the breath out past the larynx and through the throat and into the ears of your lovely and delighted listeners.

THESE ARE FANTASTIC TIPS TO ADD INTO OUR
CONFIDENCE TOOLBOX!

In a world of more than eight billion people, isn't it amazing to think each one of us has our own unique voice? Some of us talk more **SOFTLY** and S L O W L Y, and some of us talk **QUICKLY,** **LOUDLY,** and **EXCITEDLY.**

WOULDN'T IT BE BORING, STRANGE, AND ALSO CONFUSING IF WE ALL SOUNDED THE SAME?

This is also true for cartoon characters!

One of the shows I voice in is CBeebies *Alphablocks*, where each letter of the alphabet is its own separate character.

I am eight of the letters—**A, B, F, G, H, O, P, W**—so I had to come up with eight different voices and accents for this show.

I remember the awesome voice director and series creator Joe Elliot asking me:

LIZZIE, WHAT DO YOU THINK LETTER **O** SHOULD SOUND LIKE ?

Each character has its unique way of speaking. They couldn't all speak the same way, or the show would get very confusing! **P** has a high squeaky voice and high energy. **G** has a slower and much lower sound. They all speak differently—just like us humans!

SO, DON'T FORGET TO EMBRACE AND ENJOY THE UNIQUENESS OF YOUR OWN INCREDIBLE INSTRUMENT!

♡

PRACTICE LIKE AN ONLINE PRO!

Are all the successful YouTubers in the world just super-confident geniuses who never make mistakes as they ask you to "like, share, and smash that subscribe button"?

I used to watch these YouTube videos and think, "Wow, they're so slick and polished! How do they just talk for so long with no mistakes?" Then one day, I met a YouTube presenter with approximately a gazillion subscribers and watched her put a video together.

I WAS SHOCKED!

She spent many hours preparing the video before it went live. She had written a script, memorized it, then practiced and practiced it until it was almost perfect. Then, she spent more time finding the right location.

YOU SEE, WE VIEWERS ONLY GET TO SEE THE SLICK AND SHINY RESULT.

Had she used the first take or read her script before she corrected the mistakes, she would've come across to the audience as a completely different, unprepared, and nervous person instead of the star that she was in the final product. Practicing and improving the script over

and over again didn't just help her video look better, it helped her relax as well.

THIS IN TURN HELPED HER SPEAK MORE CONFIDENTLY.

It's the same for class presentations or learning lines in a school play.

THE MORE YOU HEAR YOURSELF REPEAT THE LINES, THE LESS EFFORT IT TAKES. WITH ENOUGH PRACTICE, THE WORDS COME OUT LIKE A FAVORITE SONG YOU'VE LISTENED TO MANY TIMES.

Some people call this muscle memory. Scientists say that when we repeat something many times, we build a neural pathway for it, enabling us to recall and repeat it without having to think hard. I'll come back to the subject of muscle memory later.

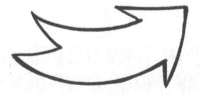

I remember when I auditioned for the part of Uniqua in the UK version of the popular US show *Backyardigans*. How would I bring this iconic pink adventurer to life as a British character and still keep her personality the same as in the US version of the show?

I tried voicing Uniqua with a low northern English accent (a bit like the singer Harry Styles). Then, I tried voicing her with a soft Irish accent (like Luna Lovegood's from *Harry Potter*) Eventually, I settled on a bright and slightly squeaky southern English accent (think a higher pitched Hermione Granger from the same movie). I needed that practicing time.

GETTING IT WRONG AT FIRST HELPED ME GET IT RIGHT IN THE END.

Now, I can't imagine hearing Uniqua speaking any other way. And let's not forget to mention her bestie, Austin! It took me a while to get his voice right, too. He is shyer than the other characters, and it was important to reflect this in his voice by making him sound a little softer and a little less confident. I still get letters from young people telling me that they relate to Austin.

THAT'S THE POWER OF THE VOICE!

Receiving letters like these make all that practice worthwhile!

Mega-star Harry Styles does tons of performing, both onstage and in movies. He looks and sounds confident, but even Harry has admitted to having anxiety and getting nervous sometimes. At his mom's wedding, he gave a speech to 100 people at a restaurant and described it as **"THE MOST NERVE-WRACKING THING I'VE EVER DONE."** Yet he was able to pull it off, saying that practice helped. **"I PRACTICED ON MY OWN FOR DAYS BEFOREHAND, AND ON THE SOFA RECITING IT TO MYSELF."** Seems this practice thing works!

When I am asked to audition, I like to read the script out **LOUD** in **LOTS OF DIFFERENT WAYS** and in different voices.

The brief I'm given might say:

YOU'RE AUDITIONING TO VOICE A 40-YEAR-OLD GIRAFFE FROM SCOTLAND.

But when I get to the studio, the director might say:

HE'S NOT A GIRAFFE ANYMORE. NOW SHE'S A 10-YEAR-OLD SQUIRREL FROM NASHVILLE.

Good thing I practiced lots of different ways!

Once, I auditioned for the part of a cute 10-year-old hedgehog, and the instructions said she needed to speak with a Liverpool accent (the same accent as the British band the Beatles). Because sounding like a hedgehog is not something I do every day in my normal life, I started practicing. I imagined this small, cute creature couldn't possibly have a low voice, so I made it higher. I spent a few minutes every few hours each day, trying to get it right. **REPEATING IT OVER AND OVER** meant reading the script got easier, and my Liverpudlian hedgehog voice was perfect.

It was totally worth the effort because I got the job, and I also had fun creating the voice and character. (My hedgehog's name was Jude—hey Jude!)

Even when practice doesn't get us what we want, we can still feel happy knowing we really tried. And, if we make practicing fun, we can feel happy that we had fun trying!

WHAT IF IT'S NOT FUN? WHAT IF IT'S TOO HARD TO PRACTICE? WHATIF, WHATIF...

WHATIF, YOU'RE TRYING TO MAKE ME DOUBT MYSELF AGAIN! THERE IS ALWAYS A WAY TO MAKE PRACTICING FUN!

One time, I felt really unwell before an audition, but I wanted to act in that show, and I was not going to miss my chance. I made it to the studio and did my best, but I hadn't been able to practice at all because I'd felt so sick. I didn't get the job. **COINCIDENCE?** Maybe, but I can tell you it wasn't a walk in the park speaking into a microphone and trying to experiment with voices while not feeling prepared. I'm sure the director wasn't impressed.

MAKE PRACTICE FUN

TIP 1

Practice doesn't have to mean spending hours sitting at your desk. It can be as simple as reading through your lines when you have a couple of minutes on your own. **TRY TO MAKE PRACTICING FUN!** First, imagine how you'll say it and how you will stand. Then, act it out. You can do this anywhere—in the shower or even while riding in a car or doing chores.

TIP 2

Practice your lines in front of a mirror. This way, you can see how others will see you. We humans have a natural tendency to copy or "mirror" each other. If you look miserable, your audience might start looking miserable too.

SO, PRACTICE SMILING TO HELP YOUR AUDIENCE RELAX! You'll be amazed at how much friendlier your audience will seem.

TIP 3

PRACTICE IN FRONT OF SOMEONE YOU TRUST.
You could ask them if they would listen to you speaking the lines. Then, ask them to tell you something they think you're doing well and something you could add or take out to make it even better. See if you should speak more slowly or pause more often to let your audience catch up with what you're saying.

TIP 4

If you really don't want people to hear you practice, say your lines on your own or to your favorite stuffed animal—admit it, we all have one. Mine is a monkey named Gregory.

HOWEVER YOU LIKE TO PRACTICE, THE KEY IS TO DO A LITTLE AT A TIME, BUT OFTEN.

I promise you, the more you repeat it, the easier the words will come, the better you'll feel, and the happier you'll be with your performance.

Which brings me to a tip from one of my fellow CBeebies *Alphablocks* voice actors!

★ TIPS FROM THE TOP ★

DAVID HOLT

VOICE ACTOR

Hi, my name is David Holt, and I'm a professional voice actor. You might know me as the voice of **7, 9, 14,** and **17** in the fabulous series *Numberblocks*. And I've done countless other voices in more than 100 animated series and lots of films over a very long career. Now, my top tip for speaking in public or recording your voice is to always be familiar with your script. Only if you're confident with the words can you deliver a smooth, assured, believable performance that will really make people sit up and take notice of what you're saying. So, practice by reading! Read everything and read aloud. Read to yourself and read to friends.

Polish your reading skills. That way, you can turn a piece of text on a page into speech. It's what we call **"LIFTING IT OFF THE PAGE."** It's what I do all the time.

IT'S MY JOB, AND I ABSOLUTELY LOVE DOING IT!

What an amazing tip for our **CONFIDENCE TOOLBOX!** Thank you, David.

IF YOU CAN THINK OF MORE IDEAS TO #MAKEPRACTICEFUN, LET ME KNOW!

Being prepared and practicing isn't just helpful for speaking, it builds confidence for any kind of performance.

SUPER SOCCER LEGEND Lionel Messi knew that

to be really confident, his talent needed to be met with some hard work practicing his skills. The same is true of the amazingly talented ballerina Catherine Conley. She made headlines globally when she became the first American to study at the world renowned Cuban National Ballet School. Catherine then went on to join the legendary National Ballet of Cuba. Catherine told me, "Much of my confidence comes from being really prepared and knowing I've done everything possible to perfect my performance."

LIVING THE VR DREAM

I'm going to share a tip I use just before I start a recording session. You can use it at any time. It's a good one for the toolbox if the thought of giving a class presentation or speech or reading in front of others fills you with dread.

BEFORE YOU START SPEAKING, IMAGINE YOU'RE PUTTING ON A SPECIAL VR HEADSET.

This headset takes your imagination into the future. Once you have put it on, imagine the headset asking you (in a very calming, futuristic robotic voice):

HOW WOULD YOU LIKE TO FEEL AT THE END OF THIS SPEECH OR PRESENTATION?

How would you reply?

Perhaps you'd say something like:

I WANT TO FEEL RELAXED AND HAPPY AND THAT I'VE DONE MY BEST. I WANT TO HAVE HELPED MY AUDIENCE, AND MAYBE EVEN GET A ROUND OF APPLAUSE FROM THEM.

Then, start to imagine what that looks and feels like.

IT FEELS GOOOOD, RIGHT?

But how can you actually get to that point?

(By the way, you can take the headset off now.)

WHY IS THIS IMAGINARY VR HEADSET USEFUL? Because it allows us to imagine a positive outcome and picture how our speech can go really well.

Another visualization technique that can be helpful is to imagine you're wearing a special suit of armor. I call it the **ARMOR OF RESILIENCE!** It's easy to wear (because it's imaginary), plus it looks great. If you imagine that you're wearing a really cool suit of armor that makes you feel strong, it can help you feel more confident. **GIVE IT A TRY!**

I HATE PUBLIC SPEAKING.
OR, TO BE MORE PRECISE, I
DON'T LIKE SPEAKING TO AN
AUDIENCE SITTING IN FRONT
OF ME THAT I CAN SEE IN
REAL LIFE. I DON'T MIND
ONCE I AM GOING, BUT
WAITING IN THE WINGS TO
GO ON IS DREADFUL.

This is a quote from Richard Quest, the energetic business reporter from the news channel CNN. Even though he feels nervous about speaking in front of a live audience, he has no problems at all speaking in front of a camera with millions of people watching—go figure! This shows how even for people whose job it is to present, report, sing, or perform in front of people, these things can still feel scary. And some people find certain situations more daunting than others.

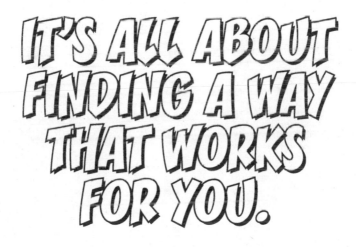

IT'S ALL ABOUT FINDING A WAY THAT WORKS FOR YOU.

CHAPTER

P IS FOR PAUSING!

The great English actor Sir Ralph Richardson once said:

"THE MOST PRECIOUS THINGS IN SPEECHES ARE PAUSES."

I was so surprised to hear this! I'd always assumed that the most important thing about speeches is **WHAT** is said, rather than **HOW** it's said. However, more and more research appears to suggest that it's the other way around! And when you think about it, it makes sense. I also need to speak clearly and pause when I'm doing continuity announcements on TV, such as:
"Coming up next on Tinypop (paaause...) it's *Mush-Mush and the Mushables.*"

I learned the importance of pausing when I got to be the UK voice of Franklin the Turtle. He's a kind little dude and always listens to his friends, so I had to make that come across to the audience through pausing and allowing his buddies to hear him properly.

Speaking of allowing your audience to hear you properly—can you imagine if at 10:56 p.m. on July 20, 1969, astronaut Neil Armstrong had put his left foot on the moon and said those famous words **"THAT'S ONE SMALL STEP FOR MAN, ONE GIANT LEAP FOR MANKIND"** in a rushed and garbled way?

"That'sonesmallstepformanonegiantleapformankind." Doesn't sound quite right, does it? If he'd said it this quickly, there's no way that sentence, which is now one of the most famous sentences of all time, would have carried so much meaning and emotion.

What if former president of the United States John F. Kennedy had rushed through this powerful, historic, and inspiring quote:

He was challenging every American to contribute in some way to the country's overall welfare and progress. He couldn't throw the words out casually, as if he were at a drive-through asking for a burger and fries!

JOHN F. KENNEDY KNEW THAT EACH AND EVERY WORD OF HIS SPEECH CARRIED WEIGHT AND IMPORTANCE.

After all, the whole world was listening to him!

Kennedy managed to give real depth to **EVERY, SINGLE, WORD.** Even now, listening to that speech gives me goosebumps because the way he says it is **SO POWERFUL!** (If you've never heard it, you can find it on the Internet. It's definitely worth a listen, especially if you need inspiration before giving a speech to your class!)

Many other leaders have developed this amazing skill of being able to speak out loud effectively. A skill like this no doubt helped them become leaders. But the good news for those of us not quite yet at the J. F. Kennedy level of public speaking is that even he had to **PRACTICE!**

This is the same with a lot of today's leaders around the world or celebrities who talk to a camera. **EVEN IF THEY MAKE IT LOOK EFFORTLESS, NO ONE KNOWS HOW MANY HOURS THEY'VE SPENT TRAINING TO DO THIS.** (This type of training is called "media training.")

So, what if we ordinary people could use a little of that special media training in our everyday life? Wouldn't it be nice to feel a little more in control when standing in front of an audience?

Well, the good news is that you don't have to pay for this special training. You can just read on for more tips!

PAUSE FOR YOUR CAUSE!

Now, if you're anything like me, the idea of pausing ...

... just feels weird and unnatural (see what I mean?).

Sometimes, we hear our friends or YouTube and TikTok stars talking so fast that the idea that anyone would take a moment of complete silence feels odd!

BUT PAUSING CAN ACTUALLY HELP US SOUND MORE IN CONTROL!

And guess what? It doesn't just help us when we are speaking. It helps the people we are talking to as well! A win for everyone!

Read each of the following words out loud really slowly if you can, pausing between each word:

NOTICE - HOW - MUCH - YOU - LISTEN - TO - EACH - WORD - WHEN - YOU - DO - THIS.

Pauses give our listeners time to really take in what we are saying and make sure they understand it, especially if they are far away from us at the back of the room.

I've had to give speeches both in real life and in cartoons. A fun example is when Henry is addressing his loyal subjects. You can hear him pausing after each line, which allows his listeners to hear him and makes what he's saying sound more important!

IF HENRY CAN DO IT, YOU CAN TOO!

LEAVE OUT THOSE FILLERS

Do you want to know what one of the biggest secret stumbling blocks when you're trying to speak out loud to other people and get your point of view across?

IT'S TIME TO MEET THE VERBAL FILLERS! *Introducing words like errrrrm, y'know, like, errrrrrr, huuuhhh, riiight, ummm, wellll, sooo, uhuhhh, and plenty more! These little fillers are sure to disrupt your flow anytime you speak. Available now in all human beings!*

Fillers are those random not-quite-words that just come out of our mouths but don't add any meaning to what we are saying. I'm sure you have used a few of these and maybe even have your regular favorites. Mine is "erm." I'm still working on trying to say this word less! Once these pesky little fillers start popping out, they become a habit, and it can be really hard to, uhhh, talk normally again when you need to say something important, y' know? They can make you sound a bit stumbly and less confident.

IF YOU THINK ABOUT IT, WE USE FILLERS A LOT, DON'T WE?

But why does our brain let us blurt out these weird little non-words?

I spoke to the very clever Professor Michael Handford, a professor of applied linguistics and English language at Cardiff University, about these fillers and asked him why we use them so much. He told me this:

> In everyday life, we use these fillers as part of our normal conversations with our friends and family, and using them is OK! It's a totally normal part of speaking.
>
> They can even make us sound friendlier sometimes. Imagine, for example, that you've invited a friend to a party. Which reply sounds friendlier?

1 "No, I can't come to the party."

OR

2 "Er, no, I, erm, can't come to the party."

> Number 2 sounds a bit friendlier, doesn't it? It sounds like the person has given time and thought to their answer instead of just saying no.

And sometimes we find ourselves **SEARCHING FOR THE WORDS** we want to say but can't think of, and instead of just stopping talking and pausing, which can feel ... **AWKWARDDDDD**..., we keep going. We feel the need to say something, anything, to make us feel a little more, err, comfortable in that situation (see what I did there?). So, it's good to know from an expert that this is actually pretty normal. Thanks, Professor Handford!

The problem with these fillers is that if we have to deliver an important speech or presentation about something we may really care about (like climate change, for example), these non-words can make us look more **NERVOUS** and less prepared. If you watch famous people being interviewed, they never seem to use many fillers at all. Is this because they just naturally speak fluently? Definitely not! Like the YouTube stars we talked about earlier, celebrities know that what they say can

influence a lot of people. They have **PRACTICED** and had coaching on how to avoid using these words.

They've understood that using these little pesky fillers can make their words less impactful.

So, how do we stop using fillers in those important speeches or presentations?

CHECK OUT THESE TOOLBOX TIPS...

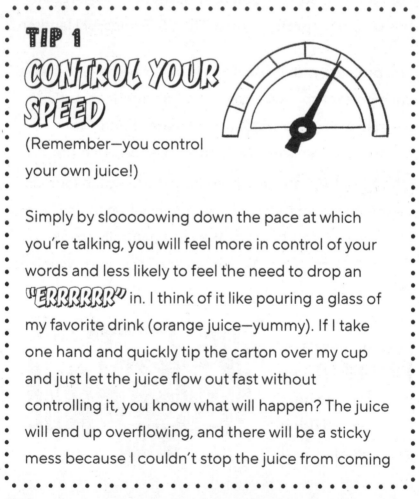

TIP 1

CONTROL YOUR SPEED

(Remember—you control your own juice!)

Simply by slooooowing down the pace at which you're talking, you will feel more in control of your words and less likely to feel the need to drop an **"ERRRRR"** in. I think of it like pouring a glass of my favorite drink (orange juice—yummy). If I take one hand and quickly tip the carton over my cup and just let the juice flow out fast without controlling it, you know what will happen? The juice will end up overflowing, and there will be a sticky mess because I couldn't stop the juice from coming out in time! But if I hold the carton with two hands and slowly pour the juice, it flows out at a nice pace, and I'm in full control—no overflow! Simply slowing down the speed of your talking will make you feel more in control of what you're saying and how you're saying it, meaning less wordy spillage!

TIP 2
THE POWER OF PREP!

Yes, it's that word again: **PRACTICE!**
In case you missed it the first time, *practice* means "to perform something repeatedly in order to improve it." Now, I don't mean just practicing for important presentations or school plays or, in Henry's case, practicing his air guitar.
You can practice talking for any time you know you are going to have to talk to someone new. Some of us find talking to new people easy and can chat away with no problem. Others get really nervous. I'm going to let you in on a little secret I'm calling...

LIZZIE'S SECRET PHONE BEHAVIOR!

As you know, my job is to talk. I like to think I can happily talk to anyone face to face without getting nervous. (Well, except for the time I got to read lines with one of my favorite actors, Richard E. Grant, when we were voice recording *The Jungle Book: The Mowgli Stories* for Audible. I got a little starstruck!) Sometimes though, for no reason at all, I get nervous when I see my phone ring, even if I recognize the number. Go figure! And sometimes, when I know I've got an important phone call coming up, and I have to tell them some important information or explain something specific, I can start to feel a little anxious and worried I won't get the words out right. I thought maybe I was the only person who experienced this, but after doing some research, it seems this is an actual thing called **TELEPHOBIA.** Who knew?!

It made me feel much better that it wasn't just me who sometimes felt this way about my phone. It also made me realize that all of us experience nerves in different situations, which should make us feel a little less alone! Maybe you get nervous when talking to your friends online or when you have to walk into a birthday party.

HOPEFULLY IT HELPS TO KNOW THAT THIS IS NORMAL!

One day, I got so nervous about an important call, I started to write down all the things I had to say to that person before the call began. I then went further and made it into a little script, guessing what they would say in reply. Then, I practiced reading my script alone before the call, and this helped. By the time the call came, I was so much more prepared and relaxed, and I managed to get the information out without the other person even realizing I was reading from a piece of paper.

I'D PRACTICED THE WORDS ENOUGH

to sound relaxed and natural. I still use this trick and recommend it to anyone who stumbles a bit on phone calls!

I can remember one time being asked to voice lots of animals in a new cartoon. The director said:

LIZZIE, WE NEED YOU TO TALK USING REALISTIC ANIMAL NOISES, BUT WITH REAL WORDS.

This was confusing to me. I've yet to meet an animal that speaks using actual words, so how on earth do you talk like a dog in a realistic way?

I could feel myself panicking. The director said:

OK, DOG FIRST!

I breathed in and shouted:

WOOF WOOF, PLEASE TAKE ME FOR A WALK!

NOW, CAT! HAMSTER! MOLE!

I started PANICKING, which made me stumble and use those annoying fillers, which interrupted my attempts at animal language. My little zoo of animals began to sound very weird. My efforts did not impress the director one bit, and they ended up asking my colleague to do those animal voices instead. I can laugh about it now. Since then, I've done hundreds more animal voices and would

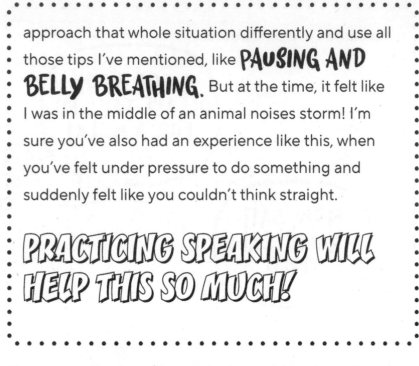

approach that whole situation differently and use all those tips I've mentioned, like **PAUSING AND BELLY BREATHING.** But at the time, it felt like I was in the middle of an animal noises storm! I'm sure you've also had an experience like this, when you've felt under pressure to do something and suddenly felt like you couldn't think straight.

PRACTICING SPEAKING WILL HELP THIS SO MUCH!

Someone who has a fantastic tip on this subject is actor Jules de Jongh. Meet the star of the awesome international Emmy® award nominated cartoon *Mush-Mush and the Mushables,* in which I voice Bolly and Miff.

★ TIPS FROM THE TOP ★

JULES DE JONGH

VOICE ACTOR

I'm Jules de Jongh, and I do **LOTS** of voices in cartoons and games. And I go out and talk to crowds of people as well. You want to know what I do to prepare for giving a talk? I type out exactly what I want to say and how I want to say it. And then, I **PRACTICE!** First, I read it in full. Then, as I get better, I start turning words that I don't need to read in order to remember to white, so I can't see them. I usually start with words like **"THE"** and **"AND."** As you practice, you can start removing more and more words until all you're left with are the few you need to spark your memory. And once you get to that point, you don't need to say the speech word for word.

IT'S BETTER TO BE MORE GENERAL, GETTING THE IDEA ACROSS IN A RELAXED WAY, THAN WORRYING ABOUT SAYING THE EXACT WORDS YOU ORIGINALLY WROTE DOWN.

And here's someone else who understands the power of engaging your audience. Actor Jimmy Hibbert is a cartoon voiceover legend who voiced Dylan the Rabbit from *The Magic Roundabout*. Here he is to give us another top tip for our toolbox...

★ TIPS FROM THE TOP ★

JIMMY HIBBERT

ACTOR

Dylan the Rabbit here, of *The Magic Roundabout*. I'm not great at public speaking, but I've had one or two tips from a voice actor named Jimmy Hibbert. He's been in the business for 40 years and says he knows a thing or two about errr, like, errm, things. So, like, one of these, you know, like, things like is, well, you know like to stay clear of using like unnecessary words like, well like, and well, and, you know. And so to start a sentence, it's like best to work out what you're gonna say before you start saying it. Because if you keep stopping in the middle of what you're saying, you're gonna, like, bore the people you are talking to. Speaking of boring, that's another thing. Jimmy says I can bore a hole in a carrot, and if you want people to listen to you, he says you gotta sound interested in what you are telling them about. Not drone on and on like a boring old carrot.

THANKS DYLAN AND JIMMY!

The more you can practice talking out loud, the better you'll get at it. And practicing doesn't mean just talking, you can practice by rapping or singing with your friends.

Now that you're aware of fillers, you'll be amazed at how often you notice people using them! And don't worry if you find yourself slipping them in accidentally—as Professor Handford said, it's normal!

THE POWER OF YOUR VOICE'S REMOTE CONTROL

Would you follow a YouTuber who spoke so fast you could hardly understand what they were saying? No, me neither. Now, don't get me wrong, sometimes speaking fast is a good thing. We sometimes speak fast when we are excited about something, like when you want to share some amazing news with your friends or family. Speaking quickly means you're passionate or excited.

In *Mush-Mush and the Mushables*, I voice Bolly, who talks supersupersuperfast. He's a speedy little guy who zips around at what seems like 100 miles per hour and gets very excited. Talking quickly really helps bring out his fun, zippy personality and high energy.

My biggest **SPEED** challenge was to say the alphabet backward in less than five seconds! Now, I could read the alphabet backward fine off a piece of paper quickly, but to say it in under five seconds would mean lots of practice and using muscle memory. I started by writing the letters out like a poem, in readable chunks. I then read these 26 letters backward over and over and over again, until gradually I started to remember them. I grouped the letters together like this:

ZYXWV
UTSRQP
ONMLKJ
IHGFED
CBA

Grouping information like this really helps me learn little bite-size chunks one at a time rather than all at once. You can do this with any info you're given that you need to learn. I realized that my little chunks sounded like a rhyme, so I started practicing it like that. After many, many tries, I'm proud to say I can recite the alphabet backward in under three seconds!

One of my favorite parts of my job is voicing characters in video games, whether it's aliens, avatars, or additional enemies. I've voiced lots of unusual characters.
I remember my first big gaming audition in London.
I'd voiced tons of cartoons but was new to video games and was **NERVOUS.**
I asked the director:

DO YOU HAVE ADVICE ON HOW FAST OR SLOW, QUIET OR LOUD THE CHARACTER SHOULD SPEAK?

His reply was amazing and shaped the way I voice all my characters now. His advice went something like this...

> **"** Unless you're shouting in a battle scene or in some extreme situation, speak as if you were in a normal conversation. The players are listening to you throughout the whole game and will get bored or lost if you constantly speak too slowly. Equally, they won't understand you if you speak too quickly. Save getting louder or quieter for those moments when you really want the audience to listen.
>
> This will make the game way more fun and engaging for everyone. Think of your voice like a game controller that you have the power to control. **"**

THIS ADVICE MADE ME FEEL INSTANTLY MORE RELAXED, BECAUSE IT REMINDED ME THAT WE ARE ALL IN CONTROL OF OUR OWN VOICE.

Whenever we feel ourselves speeding up, especially when we're nervous, or talking too slowly when we feel bored or tired, it really comes across to whom we are talking. And let's face it, no one wants their audience to feel confused, frustrated, or bored!

SO, HERE ARE A FEW SIMPLE TIPS FOR OUR TOOLBOX ON PITCH, SOUND, AND SPEED.

TIP 1

Take a **DEEP BREATH** before you start speaking. This will instantly help you feel more comfortable and ready to talk.

TIP 2

If you realize you are talking really, really quickly, just pause and ask your listeners if you're talking too fast. Or simply say:

> HOLD ON, I'M SPEAKING TOO FAST. LET ME SLOW DOWN.

Or, you could say to them:

> I AM A FAST TALKER, SO LET ME KNOW IF YOU DON'T UNDERSTAND, AND I WILL SLOW DOWN.

TIP 3

SIP WATER!

A great trick when you're speaking too quickly is to have a glass of water next to you. When you feel you're speeding up or are losing control of your words, taking a sip of water helps pause the conversation. This trick can be used every day with your friends, as well as when you're giving a presentation.

TIP 4

If you feel you talk too slowly, practice reading chunks of your favorite book out loud at different speeds, either to yourself or to someone you trust. This can help you get your mouth and eyes used to working together faster.

TIP 5

Another fun trick for speeding up talking is to practice some **TONGUE TWISTERS.** For example, greek grapes, greek grapes, greek grapes. This helps strengthen the muscles you use when you talk and helps your words come out fluently.

People may not recall everything you said, but **THEY WILL REMEMBER HOW YOU MADE THEM FEEL.** That comes from the way you say the words. Think about how passionately Greta Thunberg delivers her speeches. Another example is Taylor Swift. Every time I hear Taylor singing "Shake It Off," I smile because I can tell from her voice that she's loving the words she's singing!

BE PROUD OF YOUR LOUD!

I have to do a **LOT** of yelling and shouting when I voice cartoons and video games. This is because a lot of my characters have really **HIGH ENERGY,** and I need to communicate that to the audience. But if I'm voicing a quieter or shier character, like my buddy Austin in *The Backyardigans*, speaking quietly helps his personality come out. In the same way that you use your TV or tablet remote control to adjust the sound, the volume of how you speak can really help you get across what you want to say to other people.

HERE ARE A FEW TIPS TO MASTER YOUR VOLUME BUTTON!

TIP 1

STAND AS TALL AS YOU CAN. This not only helps you feel more confident, but it helps your voice project much better than if you were slouching or cowering in the corner.

TIP 2

If you're talking to a big group like your class, **DO A NICE BIG BELLY BREATH,** like the ones that Mel Churcher mentioned earlier. Doing this ensures you're speaking from your diaphragm (the big muscle under your lungs). This will help you talk from deep inside rather than your chest and will give your voice more **POWER** and volume. Your audience will be able to hear you better, and you will sound clearer and more confident.

TIP 3

OPEN YOUR MOUTH WIDE when you talk. This is an easy trick to help your voice sound louder and clearer.

TIP 4

DRINK WATER. This helps build our saliva (aka spit!) reserves. When our mouth is dry, it's hard to get words out, so the more fluid rolling around in there, the clearer our speech will sound, and the easier it is to keep our voice nice and loud. *BOOM!*

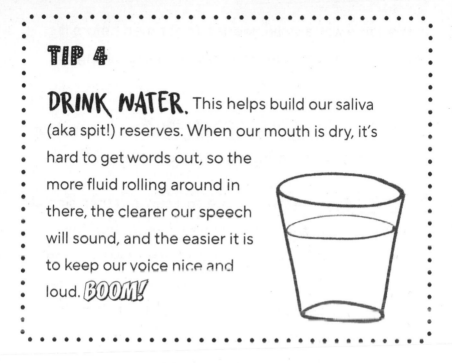

PERFECTING THAT PITCH

Pitch means "how high or low our voice sounds." My character Glenda the glittery fairy speaks in a really high voice. My character Tim in *DinoCity* talks "really low, dude." We all speak with a different pitch. Sometimes, though, we want to make sure what we are saying comes out in the clearest way, so our audience understands and remembers what we're saying.

In the same way a violin needs to get tuned before it's played, we can also tune our voices before talking to someone:

1 KEEP DRINKING THAT WATER! This will prevent your voice from sounding dry or crackly.

2 SING! Sing the lowest note you can and then sing all the way up to the highest note you can sing. This helps you understand, hear, and practice the "tone" of your amazing instrument, your voice, all at once! Plus, it warms your voice up so you don't stumble when you start speaking. Winning! And if you don't enjoy singing, just hum your favorite tune instead.

3 RECORD YOURSELF speaking and listen back to it or speak in front of someone you trust. Speaking naturally is the best way to talk, but sometimes it's helpful to ask someone you trust to tell you whether your words are coming out clearly.

SPEAK YOUR BODY POWER

Whenever I heard the words *public speaking*, I'd think "boooring." I imagined someone giving a long boring talk to a room full of bored people on a boring subject.

UNTIL...

I went to a fundraising concert and heard one of my favorite musicians of all time talking to the crowd. I don't remember what he said, but I do remember that the passion he had about the subject seemed to engage the whole crowd. He had us in the palm of his hand (not literally; that would be weird). That's how you know he was a great public speaker.

He ended up raising tons of money for the charity because he really connected with his audience. That's when I realized the power in being able to speak confidently in front of a class or a big group of people.

We will talk about rocking that class presentation later in this book, but here are a few tips to feel more confident when speaking to a group of people by just grounding your body.

TIP 1

Start by lifting your shoulders up as high as you can, pause for a second, and then release them down. Ahhhh ... this might make you feel more relaxed instantly! I call this my Mighty Mini Massage.

TIP 2

Both feet should be firmly on the ground and apart, not together, and no crossing your legs. This will keep you from falling over, and you will feel more balanced and in control.

TIP 3

Hold your head up high. You'll seem calmer and more confident.

TIP 4

Look around at the audience. This can be scary for a few seconds, but it will help build a connection with the people you are addressing so they will instantly become more like friends rather than scary people in an audience. If you can go one step further, try making eye contact with them. It will make them feel like you're talking to them individually. They will be more likely to root for you and listen to what you have to say.

TIP 5

Lots of people find it hard to know what to do with their hands when they're speaking in public. One thing you can do is keep your hands by your sides. This might feel weird or awkward at first, but it will actually make you look more relaxed. Doing this will help if your hands are shaking and will make you feel more grounded. Or, you could use your hands to emphasize important words by gesturing while you're talking. This will not only give your hands something to do but help engage your audience with what you're saying. Next time you're practicing for a speech or presentation, take some time to practice what you'll do with your hands while you talk. It could help you feel more prepared.

Here is Lizzie's **CLASS PRESENTATION RAP.** You can say it to yourself next time you get nervous about speaking out loud to a class!

Keep your FEET on the GROUND,

Do NOT walk around.

Keep your FEET on the ground and stand TALL.

Keep your HEAD held HIGH

(But Lizzie, WHY?)

'Cause THAT'S how your class presentation's gonna FLY.

You gotta SCOPE the ROOM,

You gotta LOOK in their EYES.

Don't want ANY weird FACES giving YOU a SURPRISE.

HANDS down LOW,

BREATHE in SLOW.

Put a SMILE on
your face.

You're GOOD
to GO!

SCREEN SAVERS (PLEASE, NOT ANOTHER VIDEO CALL!)

Have you ever had to talk to someone online? Maybe you have had to for a virtual school lesson or to your friends while you're playing a video game together remotely. It can feel a little weird. You're not in the same room with them, so talking to a tablet or computer can feel unnatural and uncomfortable. Well, guess what—even most grown-ups find this super-awkward. But we have to learn to embrace the tech! We need it for school, work, interviews, and catching up with friends.

Tech can be tricky even for professionals and can quit working when we really need it not to, but whether you're a YouTuber, gamer, animator, influencer, actor, scientist, or astronaut, prep is the key! No one knows this better than celebrity interviewer Katherine Schell, who has some great tips that we can use in our everyday calls. Let's gooooo!

" Hi, I'm Katherine Schell, and I'm a reporter and film critic for "Kids First Film Critics" and "Kat Around Town." I interview a lot of celebrities, and ever since COVID, I've done a lot of interviews via Zoom. Here are a couple of tips to help you get the best-quality media for your interviews. First, always do a ton of research on your scheduled celebrity and on the production itself. I put all of my key points in the script with interview questions on an online document and have it on my computer screen for reference.

I also recommend turning off and silencing anything in your house that makes noise, like your washing machine. Turn off all notifications on your devices so that nothing goes off. If you have pets like me (I have nine dogs!), be sure to find the best way to keep them as quiet as possible. If you can, switch off your doorbell so no one rings it. I would always take a few minutes to check your microphone, video, and lighting to make sure you look your best. And I highly recommend getting a camera for your computer. I also like to mark where I'm supposed to look, so it seems like I'm making eye contact with the interviewee. I hope this helps. Good luck! **99**

WOW! So many great tech tips from Katherine to add to our toolbox. And if she can manage to keep a cool head on a call with nine dogs around, you can too!

HERE ARE SOME MORE TOP TECH TIPS:

1. Make sure you have what you need to feel comfortable in your space. As I mentioned earlier, drinking water helps your voice sound better and reminds you to pause. Have some next to you so you don't have to run out for a drink in the middle of the call.

2. Test your equipment the day before the call or recording, then an hour before, then 10 minutes before. This may sound like a lot of checking, but you can't predict when a tech glitch could happen!

3. Make sure your device is charged so it doesn't die halfway through that important moment. And have a charger on standby near you.

4. Record yourself speaking to practice before your big call. Is the sound at a good level? Do you sound too loud or too quiet? You could even have a mini call with someone to check whether they can hear you well.

5. Get your angle ready. Where will you be looking? At the screen or the camera? The camera gives your audience direct eye contact, which can be great for communicating something specific, but looking at their faces on the screen might make you feel more comfortable, as you can see their reactions.

6. Is there enough light for people to see you? If you're near a window, is there a chance the sun could come out and make you start squinting? Should you close the curtain or blind just in case?

7. Will people be able to see your whole face? Having your face in the middle of the screen gives your audience a good view of you. It's hard for them to take you seriously if they can only see half of your head!

8. SMILE! It may feel weird to do that, especially if the person you're talking to isn't, but there is nothing that makes a person feel more comfortable and relaxed on a virtual call than a friendly smile.

9. During that awkward time at the beginning when not everyone has joined the call yet and there's a big pause, be brave and ask someone a question about themselves. This will help break the ice and help you all feel more relaxed, too.

10. Accept that tech glitches happen, and that's OK! They happen to everyone, even to the professionals!

Adrian Rhodes is a supervising sound editor at Warner Bros. He's the guy who places the sound in some of your favorite movies and has directed me on lots of animations, such as *Superworm* and *The Smeds and the Smoos*.

He often talks to directors and producers on Zoom calls while directing actors in the studio at the same time. Talk about logistical spaghetti! Here are Adrian's top tips for our **CONFIDENCE TOOLBOX...**

TIPS FROM THE TOP

ADRIAN RHODES

SUPERVISING SOUND EDITOR

Zoom is a tricky environment for easy conversation at the best of times. Smile as much as you can without looking demented. Speak slowly and at all costs avoid overlapping another speaker. Better to wave your hands around than to step on someone else's words! If your Zoom call drops offline, don't panic, but calmly rejoin or restart the meeting. It's always a good idea to send the other party a quick text saying you're rejoining/restarting while Zoom is doing its reboot thing.

Adrian also shared with me this golden nugget of tech advice for anyone wanting to take their sound to the next level:

To make your voice sound clearer and more present on Zoom calls, make this small change to your settings.

On the main page, go to the arrow up drop box next to the Microphone/Mute icon button on the left of the screen.

Go to Audio Settings and select Original Sound for Musicians.

Select High Fidelity music mode.

Select Echo Cancelation.

Select Stereo Audio.

WOW! Now we're all set to zoom into that conversation (well, I thought that joke was funny).

MAKING THE EVERYDAY LESS AWKWARD

Confident communication isn't just about talking. Sometimes, simply being around other people can feel a little awkward. I get to speak to lots of kids and adults on this subject, and you'd be amazed at how many young people find certain situations daunting.

Events like going to a birthday party or meeting your new baseball team for the first time can make you anxious. I still get that feeling sometimes when I start a new cartoon. It's like being at the top of a rollercoaster, when your tummy starts to feel weird. My little Whatif creature jumps back on my shoulder and whispers, "What if the cast doesn't like you, Lizzie? What if you really mess up the lines?"

Well, feeling nervous is completely normal. In fact, it would be strange if we never experienced emotions like this. It's part of being human.

I've learned that nerves are my body's way of saying, "I'm looking out for you, just do your best." The BUZZY, ANXIOUS, nervous, or excited feeling you sometimes get before doing something a bit out of your comfort zone is the stress hormone, adrenaline, preparing you for fight-or-flight mode. You may want to run away and hide from a scary situation where you feel alone or too shy to speak to someone. Sometimes, I still speak too quickly when I get nervous, and my words can tumble out before my brain has had a chance to think them through.

I still remember the first day of my first-ever voicing job, a show called *Four Eyes*! I'd never been in a recording studio before (except for the audition), so I was feeling excited, but nervous! The director and producer had flown over to England from Los Angeles, and I'd just met the whole cast that day (including voice-acting legends like Tom Clarke Hill and Jules de Jongh, who have offered us tips in this book!). When TV producer Fred Schaefer introduced himself to me, in my head I was thinking, "Act cool, Lizzie," but suddenly I got verbal diarrhea and blurted out:

Instead of sounding like a cool, experienced actor who does this all the time, I came across as a nervous newbie! Fred probably thought, "Oh gosh, she's never done a voicing job before," but then smiled at me reassuringly. Fortunately, the session went well, and we recorded 52 episodes of that cartoon! The show ended up on Nicktoons Network. I'm so grateful to producer Fred for giving me my first voice-acting job alongside such experienced actors and trusting me to do a solid American accent. So, even when we try to be cool, our nerves can take over, and our words can come out awkwardly.

I COULD WRITE AN ENTIRE BOOK ABOUT EMBARRASSING ENCOUNTERS I'VE HAD.

I remember being in a recording studio waiting room once and accidentally slamming a door so loudly, I honestly thought I'd broken it. Everyone there stopped talking and just stared at me. If only that was the end of the story... A sound engineer stopped his entire recording session and ran out to see what had happened. I wished the ground would swallow me up, but I thought I'd better pop into the recording booth to personally apologize to whoever was in there trying to read their lines. There, sitting in front of me, waiting for the engineer to restart the session I had ruined, was Sir David Attenborough, who had been narrating one of his many award-winning shows. I did that big wide goofy smile that you do when you're totally embarrassed, and I sheepishly whispered, "Sorry, Sir," and ran out. I now close doors very carefully at work! My point is, we all do stuff sometimes that makes us feel embarrassed.

So, what if there were a way we could walk into that room and manage to actually talk to someone without wishing the ground would swallow us up?

Below are some easy tricks and tools to add to our **CONFIDENCE TOOLBOX.** Try them all or pick and choose, depending on what works for you...

1. Remember, the people you're talking to could be just as nervous as you.

2. Take your time to say hello, smile, and ask the person a question. Not a question like "Why do atoms always contain the same number of electrons and protons?" But something like "How are you today?" "What's your name?" "What are your favorite ways to spend your spare time?" or "Which baseball team is your favorite?"

3. After you have asked them a question, be careful not to interrupt them while they answer. Try not to fold your arms, either, because it creates a barrier between you both, and you just look grumpy.

With these top tricks, the person you're talking to will feel like you're interested in knowing about them, and this is often how friendships begin. So, next time you're at the school playground on your own and can't see anyone to hang out with, take a deep breath and walk over to someone you don't know, with your **CONFIDENCE TOOLBOX** in hand. The more you can step out of your comfort zone, the easier these situations will become. It just takes practice!

KEITH WICKHAM

VOICE ACTOR

Hello, this is Keith Wickham. You might know me from *Thomas & Friends* as the voices of Sir Toppham Hatt, Gordon, Henry, Edward, James, and lots of other cartoon characters. My tip is to say don't drink fizzy drinks before or during a session because you'll find yourself burping and rumbling and being very uncomfortable. I hope you find that piece of information very useful. **THANK YOU AND GOODNIGHT!**

ROCKING THAT PRESENTATION.

Imagine you have to give a presentation. Picture the scene—you've done the hard work, you've written your presentation, you've practiced using all the tricks you've learned so far, and now it's time to really do it. **THIS IS THE BIG DAY!**

Just before my last year of high school, I was elected student-body president. I should add here that this honor wasn't given to me because I was particularly academic, or even a whiz on the sports field. Some of the teachers told me they voted for me because they thought I'd be good at representing the school at various events (no pressure then!). Now, despite being confident about chatting with people and performing in plays, I had not actually delivered speeches before. And one of these big speeches would be delivered to the grade above me, at the graduates' awards night, which was **A BIG DEAL!** This was a special ceremony where proud parents and guardians witnessed the graduating students collecting their well-earned achievements and awards before they headed into a new world of college or work.

My job was to deliver an eight-minute speech to the whole school, the teachers, and the parents, to inspire and encourage all the students in the year above me. I prepared by thinking of words to say (mainly on bike rides, where I always feel the most creative). Over time, I had written what I thought was a pretty good, fun speech, and I was actually quite excited to deliver it.

The night of the big event came, and my (very proud) mom ironed my school uniform and pinned my "president" badge onto my shirt. My dad dropped me off at school really early for this big occasion. He could tell I was getting increasingly nervous. When I got out of the car, he gave me a kiss on the cheek (which he always did every day before school and before any event), and he told me one of the best pieces of advice I've ever been given and still use today.

He told me to be myself and to consider two things:

1. What do you want everyone to take away from tonight?

2. What do you want the audience to feel?

(PARENT ALERT! ENCOURAGING YOUR KIDS IN THEIR SPEAKING CAN MAKE A HUGE DIFFERENCE TO THEIR CONFIDENCE!)

I rushed out of the car and headed to the school restroom to make sure I didn't have anything weird in my teeth from my dinner (you don't want green lettuce leaves stuck in your gums when you're delivering your first official speech). I could hear the cars driving into the big school parking lot and the mumblings of parents and teachers all taking their seats in the big auditorium. I looked into the mirror and took a deep breath. I had stood in front of all these students and spoken on a stage before, but not in front of parents, too, so I was feeling the pressure! But it would be OK. My speech was ready!

THEN, THE NIGHTMARE HAPPENED...

I reached into my pocket to bring out my funny, quirky, well-written speech, then realized my crumpled piece of paper with everything I was about to say wasn't there! Had I left it at home? Had I lost it on my last bike ride? I could feel myself starting to **PANIC!** I must have left it in my dad's car. He was driving home now, so I couldn't call him to check (and we didn't have cell phones back then—yes, really)! In a complete daze, I suddenly felt very alone and nervous, and I didn't know what on earth to do. I couldn't get out of speaking to everyone, and I didn't want to walk up to the principal to tell her that her student president had lost her speech for the biggest night of the school year.

After a few minutes, which felt more like a few hours, I figured I could either run away or face this disaster head on. Knowing that a few hundred people were taking their seats (gulp!), I tried to calm myself with some deep breathing. Then, I remembered my dad's advice.

I grabbed a piece of paper and a pen and started to ask myself, "What do I want this audience to think and feel from what I say tonight?" I began to scribble a few notes down. And in those eight minutes, a little revelation happened.

I SUDDENLY BEGAN TO THINK IN A COMPLETELY DIFFERENT WAY. I stopped

thinking all about me and how I was feeling and wondering how I could impress everyone. Instead, I started think about how I wanted the audience to feel. I wanted all the students to feel inspired about leaving school for their next adventure. I wanted their parents to feel proud of them. I wanted to thank the teachers who had worked hard to help them get the grades. This tiny change in my mind helped me SO much, because not being focused on myself made me feel less nervous.

So, a good tip to pop into our **CONFIDENCE TOOLBOX** right now is, the less you focus on yourself and the more you focus on how to help your audience, the more relaxed you will feel.

TOP TIPS FOR ZONING IN ON THE BIG DAY

1. You may be in your school uniform for your big speech or presentation, but if you get to wear whatever you want, make sure you wear comfortable clothes. This will help you already feel more relaxed on your special day. Think more about how your clothes make you feel rather than what you look like. The more chill you are, the more the audience will perceive this.

2. Arrive early! Whether it's your class right after lunch or an evening school event with parents coming along to watch, allow plenty of time to get to the place you need to go. You don't want to feel rushed or stressed on the way there. Allow time for hiccups like a last-minute stain on the shirt

you're planning to wear (yes, that's happened to me). Or when one of your shoes seems to disappear just as you're leaving the house, which adds on 10 minutes. (Who is that shoe thief who strikes just when you need two of them at the same time?) Allow a couple of minutes when you arrive to visit the restroom. If you can, take a minute to do your Mighty Mini Massage: lift your shoulders as high as you can, then relax them. Now, look into the mirror and tell yourself that you can do this!

3. Have a glass of water next to you and drink some before you start. Get yourself centered by switching off from the outside world or try not to think about anything else that is going on around you. That means no checking your phone if you have one—otherwise, your mind will be on

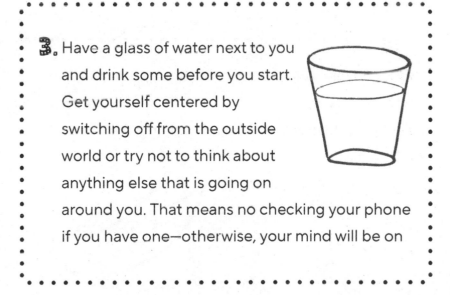

memes and weekend plans with friends. Focus on your breathing and what you want your audience to feel or take away from your talk. If they remember one thing from your speech, what should it be?

And for anyone performing on a stage, perhaps at your school or local theater or even in a TV studio, here's a great tip from screen and award-winning West End star Raj Ghatak!

★ TIPS FROM THE TOP ★

RAJ GHATAK
VOICE ACTOR

Hello, this is Raj Ghatak, one of the many voices from *Milo* and *Hilda* on Netflix. So, if I were to give you a tip, my suggestion would be to make sure you've eaten properly, because if you're hungry and your tummy starts to rumble, the microphone will pick it up. So, **MAKE SURE YOU'VE EATEN,** but try to avoid dairy or chocolate because sometimes that can create mucus in the throat. And when you go to the studio, take some snacks with you. You can take bananas, or apples are very good because they keep the moisture in your mouth. Or you can take whatever you'd like. But make sure that you do eat well, and that should also help with your concentration.

A delicious tip for our **CONFIDENCE TOOLBOX!**

CHAPTER 4

CONNECTION!

IS ANYBODY OUT THERE?

HUMAN CONNECTION is a bond that's formed between people when they feel seen and valued. During an authentic human connection, people exchange positive energy with one another and build trust. Human connection makes you feel heard and understood and gives you a sense of belonging.

Wouldn't it be great if there were a way to instantly connect with your audience before you even started speaking? Now by *connect*, I don't mean send them all a WhatsApp message from your phone or start a group FaceTime call—that would be weird. I'm talking about a way to instantly build a friendly connection with whomever you're talking to, before you've even said a word.

Well, guess what, you can! I like to call this section my

CONFIDENCE CONNECTOR TRICKS.

They're like magic tricks, so they probably won't go

right the first time, but with enough practice, they'll become easier to do and get even more effective with time. You don't have to take my word for it, as these tips come from some of the best cartoon voice actors in the world!

★ TIPS FROM THE TOP ★

WAYNE FORESTER
VOICE ACTOR

Hello! My name is Wayne Forester, and I'm a voice actor. I work in films and on television, and I've created lots of voices for cartoons and computer games, but you probably know me best as the voice of Dad in *Horrid Henry*.

Now, I have a super talking tip for you, and it's a very simple one, but it's VERY effective, and that is simply to **SMILE.** Smile before you speak and try to think about smiling when you speak. Because smiling can do magical things for you, for the people who are listening to you, and also for your voice. So, before you start speaking—simply smile.

This will help relax you. It will also be nice for the people who are about to listen to you, because they'll all think, "Ooh, this is a very friendly, relaxed person, so I'm going to enjoy listening to what they have to say." And finally, a smile does wonderful things for your voice itself without you even realizing. It makes you sound brighter and more positive. It gives what you're saying or reading a little boost, if you like, which is more interesting for everyone! **SO REMEMBER—SMILE. IT WORKS LIKE MAGIC!**

What a great tool from Wayne to add to our **CONFIDENCE TOOLBOX!** Research backs up Wayne's tip. Ready for some science?

1. SMILING MAKES YOU LOOK COOLER— IT'S OFFICIAL!

Researchers have found that people seem to be "cooler" when they smile compared to when they show a straight face. Smile and you will look more confident, even if you don't feel that confident.

2. SMILE AND THE WORLD SMILES WITH YOU

Other studies have shown that we often copy each other without realizing. So, if you're smiling at your audience, they are more likely to smile back. I'd much rather have people smile at what I'm saying than looking bored or miserable!

3. SMILING MAKES US FEEL GOOD

Seeing an audience smiling back at you will increase chemicals in your body that make you feel happy and calm. These chemicals are called *hormones*. When your brain is producing chemicals that make you feel good, it will send good vibes to your mind and your audience's minds. Ahhh, I'm feeling more relaxed already!

And remember, like all these tools, learning how to smile at a room takes time and practice. It may feel uncomfortable or unnatural at first, like when you try on a new pair of shoes. The shoes may feel a bit weird on your feet, not like your comfy old ones, but over time they will start to get worn in, and gradually they'll get so comfortable you'll start forgetting they're new! **WHY DON'T YOU PRACTICE A LITTLE NOW?** Ready? Smile at the room! There you go, keep practicing, and as the muscles get used to this movement, smiling will only get easier!

THE SECRET POWER OF YOUR EYES!

OK, so maybe you can understand the idea of smiling at your crowd, but the idea of looking around the room at the audience completely **FREAKS YOU OUT!** Perhaps you're thinking:

HOW ON EARTH WOULD LOOKING AT THE AUDIENCE HELP ME? I'M NERVOUS ENOUGH ALREADY AND DON'T NEED TO BE LOOKING AT THE VERY PEOPLE THAT I'M STRESSED ABOUT SPEAKING TO.

IF THIS IS YOU, DON'T WORRY—HELP IS HERE!

If you think about when you normally talk to a friend each day at school or perhaps at their house, you probably don't even think about the fact you're looking at them as you excitedly tell them about what you've been up to that weekend or the latest video game avatar you created. You're automatically looking directly into their eyes because you are connected to your friends, and you're keeping each other engaged in your conversation in a natural way. You're enjoying being with them, so it probably doesn't even cross your mind that you're looking at them! (By the way, if you don't normally look at people in the eyes when you're talking to them, now is a great time to start. It really helps build this connection with someone.) **BY SIMPLY LOOKING AROUND THE ROOM, YOU WILL MAKE YOUR AUDIENCE FEEL MORE RELAXED AND FOCUSED ON WHAT YOU'RE SAYING!**

EVER TAKEN THE TIME TO LOOK AT THE PICTURE ON A CEREAL BOX? Depending on the type of cereal you like, it's often a cartoon character. Does it feel like the character is looking directly at you? If so, this isn't by accident! Researchers at Cornell University carried out a fascinating experiment.

They showed a group of people two cereal boxes with a picture of the same cartoon rabbit on the front. On one box, the rabbit was looking away from the viewer, but on the other box, the rabbit appeared to be staring right back into the eyes of anyone looking at the cereal box. The experiment revealed that when the picture of the rabbit looked directly into people's eyes, it made them feel more connected with the rabbit, which made them feel more confident about trusting the cereal company. This shows the power of **EYE CONTACT!**

And speaking of cereal cartoon characters, here's a tip on this subject from the voice of one of the most iconic cereal commercials of all time, the original Kellogg's Frosted Flakes Tony the Tiger! (This was one of my favorite commercials when I was a kid, so to have the voice of one of my heroes in this book is a real honor.) Take it away, Tom Clarke Hill!

★ TIPS FROM THE TOP ★

TOM CLARKE HILL

VOICEOVER ARTIST

Hi kids. My name is Tom Clarke Hill. You younger ones might know me as Mangle the robot in *Robozuna*. You older kids might know me as Tony the Tiger for Kellogg's Frosted Flakes. Now, my big tip for being able to talk to groups of people was taught to me when I first started doing acting. A lot of people get nervous when they see the camera staring at them. And what I do is picture my best friend in the lens, a guy named Robbie, and I just deliver the lines for the script or whatever I have to say to my buddy Robbie! Which in a real situation I would do as relaxed, normal, and there would be no fear or anxiety. And I'll end with what my grandmother used to tell me too. My granny was a concert pianist, so she used to perform in front of thousands of people. And when I would feel a little insecure about doing something, she would say, "Honey if not you, WHO?"

SO, GET OUT THERE AND FOLLOW YOUR DREAMS.

In other words, we all have something unique to offer the world! This really is superstar advice and a great tool for our **CONFIDENCE TOOLBOX.** Think of someone whom you trust, and they can become your Robbie during that presentation or video call!

I spoke to Grace, age nine, who told me:

> SOMETIMES, IT MAY FEEL LIKE MY VOICE IS CLOSING, SO I TRY TO THINK ABOUT THINGS THAT I LOVE. I ALSO TRY TO BE CALM BY THINKING IT WILL BE OK IF I MESS UP BECAUSE I WILL LEARN FROM IT.

Thinking of something or someone you love may help you feel more relaxed, because this happy feeling calms down your brain (even if it feels like your brain is on fire!).

Even if things don't go according to plan, know that you have made a connection with your audience. Give yourself a pat on the back—you have tried your very best.

One lady who had an amazing way of engaging and connecting with people of all ages without even speaking out loud was Queen Elizabeth II. In June 2022, there were special celebrations around the world for Her Majesty's Platinum Jubilee, to mark her having been on the throne for a whopping 70 years! As part of this special occasion, the Queen had tea with Paddington Bear at Buckingham Palace, and it was all recorded and watched on TV by **MILLIONS** of people.

The voice director who worked on that scene is Sharon Miller. Sharon also directs me when I am voicing Ricky in *DinoCity* and in the upcoming animation series *Isadora Moon*. Sharon has given us a wonderful tip about connecting with the audience that refers to that special Paddington scene with the Queen!

★ TIPS FROM THE TOP ★

SHARON MILLER

VOICE DIRECTOR

Hello. My name is Sharon Miller, and I'm a voice director, which means I work with actors who create the voices for the characters in animation that you see and enjoy. And I've got what I hope will be a very useful tip for you, whether you're speaking in front of a large group of people, a small group of people, or maybe in front of a microphone. And that is—always use your hands and your eyes.

Sometimes, when I have an actor in the booth recording, they can have their hands in their pockets, and they're staring ahead at the script, completely dead-eyed. And I say to them, "Take your hands out of your pockets and open your eyes wide." And when they do that, the very same bit of dialogue that was dull and flat when they had their hands in their pockets and were staring ahead becomes fun. It becomes entertaining, and it becomes a character.

So, another example that you may have seen was when our late Queen had Paddington to tea at the palace. Now, I worked on that, and it was a great privilege and joy to be part of. And one of the joys was to see how the Queen used her EYES. It was her eyes and her hand gestures that told us how much she was enjoying talking to Paddington, how much she was amused by him, and how she really was happy that he'd come to tea.

SO REMEMBER, USE YOUR EYES AND YOUR HANDS, AND EVERYBODY WILL REMEMBER WHAT YOU'VE SAID AND ENJOY IT!

And if your audience enjoys it, you are more likely to enjoy the experience too. **DON'T FORGET TO TRY TO HAVE FUN!** Now, I understand that the idea of speaking out loud may not sound fun at all—it may just sound plain scary and uncomfortable. But imagine someone you like listening to or watching, maybe on YouTube or TV. Is there something about the way they say the words or express themselves that makes you want to hear more? There may just be something that you can't explain that engages you. It's likely that this thing is a sense of passion or an enthusiasm that makes you want to hear them speak.

Another terrific voice actor from some awesome cartoons has a great tip on this subject.

OVER TO YOU, AKIE...

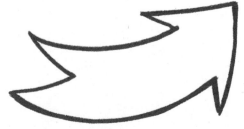

TIPS FROM THE TOP

AKIE KOTABE

VOICE ACTOR

Hey there, this is Akie Kotabe, the voice of Kyan in *Go Jetters* and other characters. One tip I have is to remember to have fun. It will go a long way! If you can imagine your audience to be a really good friend to whom you're telling a really interesting story, you'll make sure that they're getting what you're saying, everything's coming across, and that excitement and energy will carry through and no doubt affect them as well. So, what are you waiting for? Go on out there and ace it!

THIS IS A FANTASTIC TIP FROM AKIE, REMINDING US TO TRY TO ENJOY TALKING!

And it's true what they say—laughing can be infectious. Sophie Scott, a neuroscientist (someone who studies everything about the brain) from the University of

London, says, "We've known for some time that when we are talking to someone, we often mirror their behavior, copying the words they use and mimicking their gestures. Now, we've shown that the same appears to apply to laughter too—at least at the level of the brain." Sophie and her researchers played sounds to some volunteers and measured the responses in their brains with a special scanner. Some sounds, like laughing, were positive, while others were not. The response to the laughing noises was much higher than to the negative sounds, which could explain why we can't help but smile when we see others smiling. And if you think about it, having fun is contagious, and OTHERS WILL WANT TO CATCH YOUR LAUGHING BUG!

Having made people laugh for years by voicing funny characters, I can't tell you how good it feels to know you're making someone else feel happy or relaxed, even if it's only for a few minutes!

THE POWER OF CONNECTION IN A ROOM!

Sometimes, connection is like a feeling that is hard to put into words. One of the questions I get asked the most by people about my crazy job is "Lizzie, when you're recording a cartoon, do you and the cast all record the episodes separately, or are you all together in the same room?" The answer is that it depends on the show. Sometimes, I've replaced the American voices of characters like Clifford in *Clifford's Puppy Days*, or Franklin in *Franklin the Turtle*. I copy the voices that are already there, but with a British accent, so I sit and watch the episodes in a room and then follow the timing of the lines on the screen to record the voices. This is called *dubbing*.

For other shows, like Novel Entertainment's *Horrid Henry*, we record the lines first. The whole cast is in the room together as we record. IT FEELS SO MAGICAL TO ALL BE IN ONE ROOM RECORDING TOGETHER. There's a special kind of energy there. We bounce off each other's lines. We can be silly together. We can look at each other as we say the lines. We can feel the excitement in the room.

WE ARE CONNECTED. Now, if you can connect with your audience by using the tips and tools I've mentioned, such as eye contact and smiling, that connection will bring your speech or presentation to life in the same way!

Someone I've worked with a LOT is the amazing voice actor Sue Elliott-Nicholls (whom you might know better as the voice of Margaret, Henry's next door neighbor). She adds this little gem to our collection of tips on this... Get your toolbox ready!

★ TIPS FROM THE TOP ★

SUE ELLIOTT-NICHOLLS

VOICE ACTOR

Hello, my name is Sue Elliott-Nicholls, and I play Henry's sworn enemy, Margaret, in *Horrid Henry*. I'm also Andrew, Nick, the Demon Dinner Lady, and Rich Aunt Ruby. And you would have seen me on lots and lots of things on TV, cartoons, and announcing programs that are coming up. And my top tip for you is to **HAVE LOTS OF FUN!**

So, you know how when you're at the playground and you believe for half an hour that you really are a superhero, or a cat, or a big sister? And then the bell rings, and you are back to your normal self and you are going back into the classroom again. That's kind of what acting is. It's just believing that you're someone else for a short amount of time until the bell rings and you have to go back to your classroom again. So, my advice to you is have fun and play. Play with the character and keep playing imaginary games!

Another great tip! So, if it's helpful, you can try to capture the magic of pretending when you're speaking. Take yourself out of the situation for a few minutes and imagine you're performing as someone else who is really enjoying the experience, and this positivity will really translate to your audience. Thinking like this will give you confidence and help project your voice in the best way. For those few minutes, you can be whoever you want to be, which is exciting!

And someone else who also knows a **LOT** about this topic is none other than the brilliant CBBC host Ben Shires. Let's see what he says!

TIPS FROM THE TOP

BEN SHIRES

TV PRESENTER

Hello there, I'm Ben Shires, and I'm a TV host you might recognize from shows like *Officially Amazing* on CBBC. **OR** if you're really lucky, you might have managed to avoid me altogether!

SO, HERE ARE MY TOP TIPS ON PRESENTING AND SPEAKING OUT LOUD.

First, try to speak about a subject that you find really **INTERESTING,** because if an audience can hear the **PASSION** in your voice, hopefully you'll be able to transfer that emotion over to them, and they'll come along for the ride with you. It's the best way of presenting, because it means that you care about what you're speaking about.

Second, you might have heard a lot of people say if you're speaking in front of a live audience, the best thing you can do to calm your nerves is to picture that audience in their underwear. Well, I can tell you now that any large audience may include people whom you know! And the last thing that you want to be doing is picturing your Great-Aunt Petunia, or worse, your teacher, in their underwear! **SO, DON'T DO IT!** What I would advise instead is to go out there with a nice big confident voice and a smile on your face. That way, people will know that you're in control, that you enjoy what you're talking about, and that they should listen to you. And you don't even need to think about their underwear at all!

And if you feel so nervous that your mind has gone blank and you've forgotten what you're supposed to say, don't just start speaking. Allow yourself a nice, long (yes, it's this word again, ready for it?) **PAAAAAAAAUUUUUSSSSEEEEE** to give yourself time to get your thoughts together before you begin.

PRINCESS DIANA: DEVELOPING A VOICE OF TRIUMPH

It doesn't matter who you are, we are all human and have to deal with the same fears and emotions as everyone else. This included Princess Diana, who had to put a lot of work into her presentation and public speaking skills. She even had a voice coach, Stewart Pearce, who once recalled that Diana "knew that her voice was a voice of submission, not a voice of triumph. She wanted to find that." Her inhibitions started early, when Diana was a painfully shy young girl and apparently was challenged even speaking with people she did not know well. As an adult thrown into the spotlight, and after a lot of coaching, practice, and eventually getting good, positive feedback from audiences, she became confident enough to stand up for the causes she cared about. And that's another thing about passion: Diana was at ease not talking about herself but talking about causes she cared about. She knew her material inside and out, and was passionate about educating people. That made presentations something she could confidently look forward to, because she knew that her persuasion could help so many!

BREATHE AWAY THAT ANXIETY (EVEN IN A TRAIN RESTROOM)

Do you ever get asked to do something, maybe not even something that difficult, but for whatever reason, you really don't think you can do it? And suddenly that thing starts to feel so impossible and scary that you would rather shrivel up into a corner and not even try? I get this feeling too. **AND GUESS WHAT? IT'S TOTALLY NORMAL!** And in fact, according to the National Survey of Children's Health back in 2020, 5.6 million kids had been diagnosed as having anxiety, and that number is increasing each year. So, if you feel this way sometimes, know that **YOU'RE NOT ALONE!**

I often get asked to audition for some pretty wacky characters. I can look at the character description and think I can't possibly voice that and start to feel a bit anxious at the prospect of trying to find a voice. It can make me feel quite vulnerable, and so I put off doing it. **THE ANNOYING WHATIF VOICE KICKS IN BIG TIME!** "What if your voice sounds bad? What if the casting director laughs at it?"

Recently, I went on a work trip to France. I was just settling into my seat on the train (you know, the famous one that goes from London to Paris under the English Channel), when I got a phone call asking whether I would like to audition to voice the main character in a famous celebrity's new audiobook. Normally, when you do a first audition for a job, you're in a calm, quiet location where you can simply record yourself on your phone

and then send the recording over to be listened to by the casting director. This, however, was the opposite of a calm, relaxed environment. It was a busy train packed full of commuters and families.

Now, I really wanted this voice job, so trying to sound as cool as possible, I replied, "Yes, of course, I can audition, but er ... just to let you know, I am currently boarding a busy train." Inside, I was beginning to panic, thinking, **"HOW ON EARTH WILL I PULL THIS OFF?"** I jokingly suggested to the person who'd called me that perhaps I could record the script lines in the train restroom. Instead of laughing back, they simply replied, "That would be great, thanks, we're sending the script now and looking forward to receiving the clip in a couple of hours."

So, having accepted my rather unusual mission, there I was, squeezing myself into a train restroom. I was gently rocking back and forth with the train's movements, and there was that whirring noise you always seem to hear in public restrooms. I had one hand holding my phone to record myself and the other hand clutching my tablet from where I would read my lines.

I felt like giving up before I'd even started. I imagined the other actors auditioning for this role sitting in their quiet houses with the script printed out, ready to take notes, or perhaps recording the lines professionally in their fancy home studios. I thought, "This might be the worst audition I ever do." Then, I thought, "If I don't try, I will never know." I was conflicted ... I could feel my chest getting tighter.

Then, I remembered my **CONFIDENCE TOOLBOX** and knew I could find a tool that would relax me. So, I brought out my magic breath tool. This is one of the quickest and easiest ways I find to relax. It's like our **BELLY BREATHING** tip but adds some counting. To help explain what this tool is, I'm handing this little section over to the amazing voice actress Teresa Gallagher...

★ TIPS FROM THE TOP ★

TERESA GALLAGHER
ACTRESS

Hi. I'm Teresa Gallagher. You might know me as Nicole Waterson in *The Amazing World of Gumball* and lots of other cartoons and radio dramas and games. My top tip is for you to consider how important it is to **BREATHE PROPERLY.** You might say, well we all breathe without even thinking about it, so what? But when I'm feeling a bit nervous before a recording session or public appearance, I've noticed that my breathing gets really shallow and fast. It's all happening really high in my chest, but as soon as I take a few **LONG, DEEP** breaths and slowly breathe out, I not only feel a lot more relaxed, but my voice is stronger and clearer. The voice is like an engine, and the engine needs fuel, and your breath is the fuel. You need to supply the right amount of fuel to make the engine work properly. Go on, you give it a try, breathing in for a count of four and then breathing out for a count of four. That's better, isn't it? Next time you're feeling a bit anxious, give it a try! Hopefully, you will notice a big difference like I do.

Perfect advice. Our **CONFIDENCE TOOLBOX** is getting really full!

Let's go back to me inside my restroom stall! I tried Teresa's magic breath and counted **1,2,3,4.** I instantly felt calmer just from that one breath! Taking a few seconds out of a stressful situation and giving myself the time to breathe made me feel a bit more in control. I tentatively pressed the record button, and despite the various challenges, my "boy" voice began to flow out. I predicted a line of people waiting outside the restroom, so instead of my usual 20 takes, I restricted myself to two.

Having completed my mission, I opened the door to leave and saw a rather confused looking gentleman staring at me. I was wondering whether I had something weird on my face but then smiled, realizing that he must have heard my audition and expected a 10-year-old boy to walk out. I sent the recording over and guess what—I got the job! So, you never know what can happen if you take a breath and go for it.

Frankie, age 10, knows that **BREATHING** makes all the difference!

> WHEN I HAVE TO SPEAK ALOUD AND I GET NERVOUS, MY VOICE GOES DEEP SOMETIMES, AND I CONCENTRATE ON JUST BREATHING TO HELP ME GET THROUGH IT.

I'm **EXCITED** to have teamed up with Chicago City Day School and their principal, Chris Dow. Public speaking is a core part of their curriculum, and you can tell. Their students are super-confident, as they start practicing public speaking from the year they start school. If only every school did this! One student said they like to think of the audience as friends who won't judge them if they slip up during a speech. This is an excellent tip! Another asked this great question: what do you do when you're prepared but suddenly get really scared on the day of giving your speech? My advice is to use the VR technique we talked about earlier, where you picture your speech going really well, and to remember that you **WILL** get through it. Have something to look forward to after it's over.

I also had a great talk with a really fun and energetic group of students at LaSalle Language Academy in Chicago. Longtime teacher Nancy Broecker always encourages her students to speak up and ask questions. We had a fun contest where students came up with up their own cartoon character voices! I could see their confidence growing as they came in front of the group to perform.

THIS IS A GREAT WAY TO PRACTICE SPEAKING OUT LOUD IN A FUN WAY, AND MAYBE SOMETHING OTHER SCHOOLS COULD TRY!

CHAPTER

5

SPEAKING CONFIDENTLY DOESN'T JUST HAPPEN.

We don't wave a magic wand and **PING**—just like that all become amazing speakers. As you've read from everyone who contributed a tip for this book, whether they're an actor, an expert, or a young person just like you, we all can use tools and tricks to learn to communicate better. With enough practice and slow but steady changes, we can all do it, and it's totally worth it.

A couple of years ago, I wasn't even sure I had the confidence to write this book. But the more I spoke to all the brilliant people who've contributed to it, the more I could imagine how it would look and realized that we all feel nervous and unsure sometimes, even famous people! I even got to speak to students at the prestigious Yale University on this subject, some of the smartest people in the world, and even they were asking for tips on how to speak more confidently. Whether we are shy or the most talkative kid in the class, **WE ALL HAVE TIMES WHEN WE DON'T FEEL CONFIDENT, AND THAT'S OK!**

And as we've learned, it's not just speaking that can be scary sometimes. Just showing up to that class presentation, audition, baseball tryout, ballet recital, birthday party, or even just walking through the school doors some mornings can feel like a mountain that we just don't feel like climbing. Little Whatif can start chattering so **LOUDLY** that all we want to do is stay in our own comfortable place, wherever that may be. (For me, that's snuggling back under my duvet.)

But if we don't at least try—think what we may miss out on! If I'd never practiced speaking and taken that leap of faith to turn up at my first audition, I would have never become the voice of Henry in *Horrid Henry* or any of the other fun characters I've voiced over the years.

IMAGINE WHAT EXCITING OPPORTUNITIES AWAIT YOU.

So, never let your lack of confidence hold you back, even if annoying Whatif is jumping on your shoulder and whispering unhelpful things! You CAN climb that mountain—just remember to take your **CONFIDENCE TOOLBOX** with you!

So, here are my final tips for your **CONFIDENCE TOOLBOX.** Are you ready?

❄ Be kind to yourself. Talk to yourself positively, as if you were talking to a friend.

❄ Get outside your comfort zone and try something new.

❄ Realize you're not alone. Even celebrities lose their confidence when speaking sometimes!

❄ Set small goals for yourself, and over time your confidence will grow.

❄ Take it one day at a time. Some days, you might feel less brave than others, and that's OK.

❄ Finally, whatever happens, try to have fun!

YOU HAVE ALL THE TOP TIPS NOW!

You are enough! So, pick up your **CONFIDENCE TOOLBOX,** hold it tightly as you walk around, keep your head held high, and go conquer that speaking. You've got this.

GLOSSARY

ADRENALINE A hormone (which is a special chemical in your body) that helps prepare you for a stressful or dangerous situation.

ANXIOUS Afraid or nervous about what might happen.

AUDITION Try out for a part in a production, like a theater or TV show.

CONFIDENT Sure of yourself and your abilities.

DIALOGUE A conversation between two or more people.

EMBARRASSED Ashamed or shy, like you just want the ground to swallow you up!

EYE CONTACT Looking at another person right in their eyes.

GROUND YOURSELF Take a moment to feel comfortable, relaxed, and secure.

INVOLUNTARY A word used to describe an action that someone does without meaning to.

LIZZIE'S MIGHTY MINI MASSAGE Lifting your shoulders as high as you can and then letting them relax.

MIMIC Copy someone else's actions.

MUSCLE MEMORY A process in the brain that allows you to remember how to do things without really thinking about it, like riding a bike.

PSYCHOLOGIST Someone who studies the human mind and how it affects people's behavior.

PSYCHOTHERAPIST Someone who is trained to help people with their mental health by helping them talk about and understand their feelings.

RESEARCHERS People whose job it is to find out and check information, such as for a book or TV program.

VERBAL FILLERS Non-words that may appear in our speech, especially if we're nervous, such as "erm" and "y'know."

VOICE BOOTH The special soundproof room where cartoon voices and other audio are recorded.

Lizzie Waterworth had her first break into animation voiceovers aged 22, and has been voicing award-winning cartoons and video games ever since, including the lead role in *Horrid Henry* and characters in numerous successful kids' shows like *Bob the Builder* and *Mush-Mush and the Mushables*. In 2019, she was nominated for a BAFTA for her role as Henry. When she's not in a recording studio, she is helping young people to build their speaking confidence, visiting schools and businesses to run workshops, speaking at events, and coaching one-to-one. For more information visit **www.lizziewaterworth.com**

With thanks for their contributions to this book: Jenny Clarke, Emma Tate, Mel Churcher, Dr. Natalie Cawley, David Menkin, Lewis, Stephen Fry, David Holt, Catherine Conley, Professor Mark Leary, Marcel McCalla, Dr. Jane Santo, Joe Elliot, Frankie, Freya, Grace and the kids from St Thomas' C of E Primary School, Professor Michael Handford, Jules de Jongh, Jimmy Hibbert, Katherine Schell, Adrian Rhodes, Keith Wickham, Raj Ghatak, Wayne Forester, Tom Clarke Hill, Sharon Miller, Akie Kotabe, Sue Elliott-Nicholls, Ben Shires, Teresa Gallagher, Chris Dow, and Nancy Broecker.

A special thanks also to Novel Entertainment and La Cabane Productions for their contributions; Jennifer Christie at the Graham Maw Christie Agency, Dan Conley at Beacon Communications, and James, Edward & Emily.

Project Editor Rosie Peet
Project Art Editor Chris Gould
Editor Stephanie Stahl
Designer Anita Mangan
Senior Production Editor Marc Staples
Senior Production Controller Louise Minihane
Acquisitions Editor Katy Flint
Managing Art Editor Vicky Short
Publishing Director Mark Searle

Thanks to Heather Wilcox and Julia March for proofreading.

Horrid Henry™ images and references by
kind permission of Novel Entertainment Limited.
Find out more about the world of *Horrid Henry* at **horridhenry.me**

First American Edition, 2023

Published in the United States by DK Publishing
1745 Broadway, 20th Floor, New York, NY 10019

Published in Great Britain by Dorling Kindersley Limited

A catalog record for this book is available from the Library of Congress.

ISBN 978-0-7440-8312-5

DK books are available at special discounts when purchased in bulk for sales
promotions, premiums, fund-raising, or educational use.
For details, contact: DK Publishing Special Markets,
1745 Broadway, 20th Floor, New York, NY 10019
SpecialSales@dk.com

Printed and bound in the United Kingdom

For the curious
www.dk.com